ARE YOU KIDDING ME?

Amazing Occurrences in My Life

Ron Hart

ISBN 979-8-89112-764-7 (Paperback)
ISBN 979-8-89112-765-4 (Digital)

Covenant Books
11661 Hwy 707
Murrells Inlet, SC 29576
www.covenantbooks.com

To my children, grandchildren, family, and
anyone needing encouragement.

OCCURRENCES

Introduction vii

Gift from an Angel..1
Get the Kids Home—Safely!..4
Stay Focused—Your Job—Deliver the Packages 8
An Ode to My Dad 12
Who Do You Know? 17
That Embarrassing Moment—Are You Speaking to Me? 24
An Anniversary to Remember 27
Que Pasa?…Oh No, No, No 30
This Can't Be My Room 34
Nighttime Conversations...36
Thank You, Dr. V 39
Unexpected Blessings 46
    You Could Use a Hug...46
    A Sporting Gift 48
    "I Feel Good" 50
Help for the Man Dressed in Black 52
Are You Tonight's Umpire?...54
    Hi, How Are You Doing? 54
    The Catcher Did What? 55
    You Seem to Be Struggling 56
Traffic Stops and Court Visits 58
    Mr. Hart, Are You Listening to Me? 58
    Yes, I Said It 60
The Unexpected When Driving 63
    Surely, You Speak Spanish? 63
    Don't Forget to Say Grace..64

Stop—Count Your Blessings 65

Heads Up and Just So You Know… 67

Listen to That Inner Voice..69

Just Enjoying My Lunch 70

Oh, Those Awkward Moments 72

New Cellphone—Poor Excuse..72

Courtesy Is the Best Policy 73

Always Expect the Unexpected 75

I Made the Sports Page...76

Should We Always Follow Our Parents' Example? 77

Hey, Ref!...79

Oh, What a Night 84

An Introduction to Skiing 87

The Family Hits the Slopes 93

Who Is Your Teacher? 93

A Bucket List Ride 95

Down the Slopes He Goes...98

A Hart European Vacation 103

Remember to Drive on the Left..103

Please Don't Predict Anything Else 104

Now, One More Time 106

Excitement on the Tube...108

Intrigue on the Tower 110

It Must Be Christmas...113

When Santa Swore 114

A Most Remarkable Lady 117

An Upbringing in Hardship 118

Mom Being Mom 118

The Queen of Christmas..121

A Woman of Faith..122

The Longest 24 126

"Sir, Are You Okay?" 136

It Is Well 142

INTRODUCTION

Why the name *Are You Kidding Me?* for this book? This was a phrase I frequently used. I probably said it ten or more times daily.

So often, when my mother saw the phrase on a coffee cup, she stopped, went into the store, and purchased it for me. Then she would tell my sister, "This has Ron written all over it." It was the last gift I received from her, as she passed away a month later. I placed the cup in a visible location in my office until my retirement. I never used it for coffee, but it triggered many discussions.

Inside are adventures from three continents. They are unique, and many involve my family members. Over the years, I've been truly blessed and watched over in spite of myself. In the writing of the book, I was repeatedly reminded of this.

When I look back on the incredible events of my life, I just shake my head and say,

"Are You Kidding Me?"

GIFT FROM AN ANGEL

I love sports, and my favorite without a doubt is baseball. I enjoy going to the ballpark, relaxing, being with family and/or friends, and watching the game. It doesn't matter the age group of the kids or if it's professionals playing. If they are playing because they are having fun, improving, learning, and playing solid fundamentals.

Even when I watch games on TV, it's all good until they don't play fundamentals. I've been known to yell at the TV on many occasions, to cheer for the home team and celebrate winning…but not playing basic fundamentals drives me crazy and can get me out of my seat hollering… I'm going down a rabbit hole, so stop!

The Florida Marlins played their first-ever regular season game on April 5, 1993. It seemed everyone wanted to attend the first real Major League game at Joe Robbie Stadium. The atmosphere was electric as fans rolled in early; many were tailgating. The parking lot looked more like a football game was about to be played, but it was the home opener—the very first home opener. Once again, I'm getting ahead of the story…

My son, George, also enjoyed sports and attending sporting events (no surprise). He was twelve years old and in school that April day. When I arrived at his school, there was a line of parents checking out their children, most to head to the game. I remember a school official announcing no children were to be released to attend a baseball game. There was a sudden change in the room as parents in Marlin team colors were now heading to dentist and doctors' appointments. The administrator shook her head and disappeared to the back of the office.

For months, tickets for Opening Day were being sold. First, only as season tickets, then only in a multitude of bundles, finally, when individual game tickets became available, I didn't have the funds to purchase a pair, and the tickets quickly sold out. However, it was game day, we were at the stadium, parked, and I had several hundred dollars in my pocket. We should have no problem scalping and obtaining those precious tickets.

We had plenty of time before the first pitch. We hit the souvenir stands, purchased Opening Day programs, pins, baseballs, posters, and the like. We took our prized possessions to the truck to keep them out of harm's way. I was as happy as any kid anywhere and was with my son—what a great day already.

We had scalped tickets before to attend Miami Heat games and other events. I raised a hand and with two fingers, indicating the number of tickets we needed. Oh, there were tickets to be purchased, but the prices were super high, no negotiating—"Pay my price or walk on." After two trips around the stadium, I began to have serious doubts. I began telling George, I don't know if this is going to happen. He said okay, but I heard the hurt in his voice and knew there was despair in mine.

We continued to walk, my arm raised, asking for two tickets. Sellers were still asking well over a hundred dollars a ticket (more than ten times face value). Reality was beginning to set in; today was not our day. Fewer tickets were still for sale, and the prices weren't dropping. I began dad talk, telling George we had already had a good day out of school, with plenty of souvenirs, and telling him to keep the faith.

Finally, a decision had to be made under an hour to first pitch. I couldn't imagine how we would be able to enter the stadium and see all the pregame activities. The few tickets now available were being sold for much more money than I had in my pocket.

I turned to George and told him I didn't think we were going to be able to get in. Maybe we should go to the house—we could at least watch the game together. We jointly decided to give it a few more minutes. However, nothing changed; we needed to head home. I believed I really let my son down, all the excitement of game day was gone. As we walked through the parking lot, the closer to the truck we got, the more miserable I felt.

We were just yards from our vehicle when we noticed a well-dressed businessman in a suit and tie. He asked if we needed tickets to the ballgame and how many. I didn't have an arm raised or any sign saying we needed tickets, so what was happening? We replied, "Yes, sir, we needed two tickets." He asked if the tickets were for us. We again replied yes. Then he reached inside his coat pocket and handed us two tickets, saying to enjoy the game. I was stunned and speechless, but my son and I embraced, hugging one another, jumping up and down, all but crying for joy.

After several seconds, we turned to say "Thank you" and maybe hug the gentleman too, but he was gone. We looked around in every direction for him. It was getting closer to game time, the parking lot was emptying, but he was nowhere in sight, vanished, disappeared, gone!

We immediately turned around and hustled back to the stadium. I don't think my feet were touching the ground. This time, there was no stopping outside; we got to the turnstile and went directly into the ballpark.

We applauded as the band wrote "Marlins" in script across the outfield. Saw the players introduced and the American flag brought in by parachuters. Cheered on pitcher Charlie Hough and Jeff Conine, "Mr. Marlin," who went four for four, leading the Marlins to victory.

As I sat in those outfield seats and ever since, I've been so grateful for an amazing miracle and an angel who gave us two tickets to Opening Day 1993, the first game in Florida Marlins history.

I've only missed three Marlins Opening Days out of the first thirty. I'm attending with my son and now with my grandsons too. However, that first one…

The Rest of the Story

I noted I didn't have the money to purchase tickets in advance. I was working, but we had just been blessed weeks earlier with our second daughter, and her sister was only seventeen months old. We had also made a commitment to tithe our earnings. What a confirmation that our priority was in the right place.

GET THE KIDS
HOME—SAFELY!

As a youngster, I had many opportunities to play and learn sports. When my father was stationed in Norfolk, our family lived in Virginia Beach. It seemed all my friends played youth league baseball. I really enjoyed the game, although the truth be known, I wasn't a very good player.

As the seasons changed, we also played football. Although I was small in stature and weight, this was offset as the leagues were six-man and eight-man formats with weight restrictions in addition to age guidelines. Eventually, I played some eleven-man too. However, I was just too small; I made the teams but wasn't a starter, but was having fun.

I was also introduced to another round ball sport, soccer. Finally, size and weight weren't critical components to success. Chase the ball, put it in the net, and don't let the other team do so. What kid couldn't do this and get plenty of exercise at the same time.

What sports did teach, even at a young age, was teamwork and fundamentals. If you learn and apply some basic principles, you can be an asset to your team. Now as an adult, it really frustrates me to watch highly gifted players not be fundamentally sound, especially baseball players.

When I started the ninth grade, nearly all my friends were trying out for the junior varsity football team. Being that South Sumter High School was a small rural school, everyone who tried out made the team; they needed bodies. So I got the thumbs up from my dad and headed to my first practice.

I didn't even get to the locker room when Coach Hall called me aside. Asking my name, then why I was here, I proudly told him I was ready to play football. He asked what grade I was in, and I told him ninth.

Coach's hand was now on my shoulder as he said, "How much do you weigh?"

"Eighty-six pounds," I answered in my strongest voice, adding I had played football before.

He just looked down at me and said he couldn't allow me to play. Everyone on the team was much bigger; I was way too small and would surely be injured. (I did attain a hundred pounds midway through the eleventh grade).

I've started down another rabbit hole… Refocus and get back to the story.

After graduating high school, I received a scholarship as a student athletic trainer to attend Miami-Dade North Junior College. I would be under the direction and mentorship of Dave Lawson, the college's head athletic trainer. What an opportunity to be hands-on in athletic training, surrounded by sports, and yes, go to college. However, it was going to get better.

Shortly after arriving, I was assigned to work with the men's soccer team. These were outstanding, gifted players from many countries, and they could play ball. After a couple of practices, Coach Pat O'Hare noticed me kicking the ball around with some of the players and asked if I wanted to participate in the drills and join the practice instead of being on the sidelines.

My first responsibility was athletic training, but I improved my soccer fundamentals learned as a youth to the point I was listed on the player's roster, dressed, and played in games. I was at the end of the bench, played in sure wins, and even scored a goal my sophomore year. The same year, our team was ranked nationally, won our region, and hosted the National Championship Tournament, finishing fifth after losing the longest game in tournament history in seventeen overtimes.

Several of the players were involved in youth soccer around the area, but none as much as Gary. He was constantly supporting soccer. I had purchased a car before my sophomore year, which was a great benefit but also allowed me to assist others. Gary got me set up to officiate some youth league soccer games and help him with his team.

One of the first games was at night in Coral Gables, a good ride from our home base in North Miami. My Plymouth became a transport vehicle. I had five youngsters, ages eight to ten, piled into my car and the responsibility to get them from the boys' club to the game and afterward to their homes.

After the game, we got back to the car, and a tire was flat. No problem, a couple of us changed the tire, and off we went. I must set the scene. This occurred in the early seventies. There were no cell phones. It was after 9:00 p.m. As we exited Interstate 95 at Northwest Sixty-Ninth Street, a thunderstorm had rolled into the area. The boys needed to get home, and then I heard the *thump, thump, thump* of another flat tire. This couldn't be happening.

We were parked on the side of the road, flashers on, with steady rain falling with the occasional flash of lightning. I got out and confirmed we definitely had a second flat tire. The boys' laughing about another flat tire soon turned to dismay. Some wanted to walk home as they were only blocks from their house.

As time passed, I questioned what I could do. I was unfamiliar with the neighborhood and had five tired but hyped-up boys whom I really didn't know. To add to my stress, a tow truck stopped to check on us. He was on a call and couldn't help, said he'd contact his office, but added, "Be careful, this is a rough area." Nobody showed. I was steadily praying under my breath.

After nearly an hour, the rain was easing, and a policewoman pulled up. I told her our situation. She requested a tow truck, assured the boys they were going to be okay, and said she would swing back later to check on us.

Finally, a tow truck showed up. His yellow lights were a welcome sight. He assessed our situation and had several radio discussions with his dispatcher. We stood outside in light rain while the driver hooked up the car. We then crammed into the truck cab—yep, all seven of us on top of each other. The boys knew rescue was at hand and returned to being kids, laughing and enjoying the ride in the big truck.

The driver patiently drove all five boys home to their greatly relieved parents. He covered a lot of area in doing so, then he looked at me and said, "Where are we going?" I lived across town in Hialeah; we headed in that direction. Then, for the first time all night, I realized I had only a couple of dollars in my pocket, no credit card (they weren't common in the early seventies), and no access to ATMs, but maybe I could hit up my roommates for some funds.

We pulled into my apartment complex; it was well past midnight. It felt so good to be home at last. I fearfully asked, "What do I owe?"

The driver looked me straight in the eye, saying, "I've talked with my dispatcher, and after what you've been through to keep those boys safe and get them all home, we're not going to charge you!"

Wow, this was an amazing blessing and maybe I didn't fully appreciate God's watch care over my life at nineteen, but He's always been with me.

STAY FOCUSED—
YOUR JOB—DELIVER
THE PACKAGES

The more I write about the stories of my life, the more it apparent becomes how big a part sports have played.

When my dad was stationed in New York, my aunt and uncle came to visit from Pennsylvania. Uncle Howard, Dad, and I went to watch the Yankees play, it was my first major league game. The day was special and made me a Yankee fan for a few years.

A few years later, Dad took me to an NFL exhibition game in Norfolk. The Baltimore Colts were playing, and Johnny Unitas was their starting quarterback. The Colts became my team, and number 19, Johnny U. (wearing his high-top cleats), my favorite player.

After my father retired and we relocated to Central Florida, college sports became bigger focus in my young life. My mom's high school mascot was the Gators, and two of her brothers attended the University of Florida. Looking back Mom was a Gator fan even if from afar. Soon Gator football was the talk of the fall. I attended my first Gator game as a high school senior.

I remember listening to commentator Otis Boggs on my transistor radio as John Reeves and Carlos Alvarez strove to set passing records in the final game of the 1971 season. I'd run back and forth from my bedroom updating my dad. I didn't fully comprehend the Gators letting the Hurricanes score at the time. However, they got the ball; and moments later, they completed a pass and had set new national passing records.

In the excitement postgame many of the Gator players were splashing and playing in Flipper's pool in the east endzone of the

Orange Bowl. Wow, what a game—big victory and party. This proved to be my introduction to the Dolphins and the majestic Orange Bowl.

The following summer I got a scholarship to attend Miami-Dade Junior College. I was setup with a small duplex apartment from Andy Florio, the athletic department's equipment manager. This proved to be a great blessing for me. Andy had to be at work very morning ready to open the equipment room at seven. It was five miles to the college and not having a vehicle, Andy provided a sure ride each morning, although with my sports' schedule, I frequently walked home afternoon or night.

The apartment was furnished but it was bare bones and had no TV. The room was attached to Andy's home but isolated from other athletes which kept me away from many temptations. However, I had my transistor radio, it was put to good use.

It was the fall semester 1972 and a great time to be in Miami. Talk radio was popular and when not studying lessons I could be found listening to the radio, especially sports talk. There was the Munich Summer Olympics, the stealing of the basketball gold medal, terrorist attack, but nothing was taking the attention off the Dolphins.

Most Sunday afternoons, I could be found lying in bed listening to the broadcast of the Miami Dolphins. As the season progressed, so did the interest in the Dolphins. They had an undefeated season underway and were the talk of the town. The radio commentators talked of the atmosphere in the sold-out Orange Bowl, the noise of the crowd flowed into my room.

The Dolphins finished the season Undefeated and Super Bowl Champions. The only team in NFL history to go the entire season and playoffs without tasting defeat. What a story! All of Miami celebrated.

How the world turns… Just two years later, I was hired by the Baltimore Orioles as an athletic trainer, and Minor League spring training was held at Biscayne College. We used the same facilities as the now two-time Super Bowl champion Miami Dolphins. Over the course of spring training, many of the Dolphin players and staff

I had spent many Sunday afternoons cheering for were now walking through the training room saying hello to me.

All six of my spring trainings with the Orioles were held at Biscayne College (now Saint Thomas University) in North Miami. Ironically, it is located only about a mile from Andy's duplex apartment.

Let's fast forward a couple of years. In the summer of 1980, I was hired by UPS as a driver. What a blessing that was. We were expecting our first child, and I had left the university to be with my wife as it was a difficult pregnancy. It was a good-paying job, but the work was not easy, especially in a hot Miami summer.

UPS was very safety-focused, and many things I learned there have stayed with me. One of which was "All Good Kids Like Milk." But I'm staring down a rabbit hole. The primary area of my routes was downtown Miami. One afternoon, I parked the big brown truck, loaded my dolly with packages, and into the high rise I went.

I had made note that some of the packages I was to deliver were for the Miami Dolphins executive office. Yes, there was some anticipation as I entered the elevator. After a couple of normal stops, I pushed the button to take me to the floor of the Dolphins offices.

I stepped out of the elevator and was in awe. I wasn't in a hallway looking for an office; when the doors had opened, I was in the Miami Dolphins office. I was blown away; there were trophies displayed, pictures, framed front pages of the newspaper, I was surrounded by Dolphin glory and was taking it all in.

Then I heard the elevator bang shut. Desperately, I pushed the elevator button—to no avail. My dolly and all its packages were riding the elevator without a caretaker.

As with all tall buildings, multiple elevators serviced the building. As I pushed the button and waited, invariably, the other elevator door would open. Again and again, I played the game. The receptionist and several others joined in watching my game. Each time, the other door would open, sometimes with people getting off but mostly empty, and I could hear the laughter.

Finally, the correct door opened, I sprang forward to retrieve the dolly and exited the elevator to applause and laughter. I was too relieved to be embarrassed. I obtained signatures for the packages, said goodbye, and was on my way.

However, I will never forget the day I was immersed in Miami Dolphin glory, but I provided the entertainment.

The Rest of the Story

I was let go by UPS on the final day of my probation period. The only time I was ever fired. I began a forty-year career with Rinker Materials shortly thereafter, and my son was born five days later.

AN ODE TO MY DAD

My dad was a great athlete, tough, strong, and the results spoke for themselves. He never talked much about his accomplishments, but in the corner of the living room, there was a small trophy case stacked with baseball, softball, and basketball trophies. Some were for coaching, but most were for playing, and don't ever question it—he played to win.

I never saw him play in his heyday; he was selected "All Navy" in fast-pitch softball before I was born. However, I did have the opportunity to watch him play catcher and third base as a youngster. His equipment bag was frequently in the back seat of the family station wagon, which resulted in the following story:

When my father was stationed at the Naval Air Station in San Diego, California, our family lived in on-base housing. Jets seemed to be flying all the time; most kids thought about being a pilot, and we were no different. One day, while on a family car ride, my sister and I got into Dad's equipment bag. (We were probably four and five.) Finding his protective cup, we had the perfect fighter pilot air mask. While we were arguing over who was pilot next, Mom turned from the front seat, appalled, and quickly put an end to the game.

Most of my memories of my dad, the player, were of him playing slow-pitch softball in church leagues. Oh my, his bat speed… he could drive the ball. Later in life, we played on the same pickup team one summer. He was in his upper forties and wasn't very fast anymore because of his knees, but he still hit the ball farther than nearly everyone else.

Dad was a disciplinarian; you'd better listen the first time because there were probably consequences if you didn't. This usually led to lessons learned. When I was about eleven years old, I was given grilling responsibilities to watch some steaks being grilled. This was great because we didn't have steaks very often.

Needless to say, the grill got too hot, flames arose, and the steaks were badly burned. Dad quickly stepped in and retrieved the toasted steaks. He calmly instructed me on the mistakes I had made and wanted me to continue learning to grill.

However, when just a few minutes later he overheard me laughing about the blazing fire and burning the steaks to a friend, calmness was out the door. I was taken aside, told about the cost of food, the impact on the family, and that it was no laughing matter. "Bend over."

We always ate together as a family. When you put six children, Mom, and Dad around the table, there was always potential. There were unwritten rules never to be violated. Grace was always said; Mom and Dad were sincere and grateful. Mom always got a gizzard when chicken was served; she also got the first selection of whatever meat was for supper.

One evening, I was aggravating my brother, who normally sat to my left. We were having pork chops, and Dad was waving the bone in his hand while telling me to stop. I elbowed my brother once more, and Dad, becoming more emphatic, was motioning with the pork chop bone when it broke free of his grip and flew at me, striking me directly in the eye.

I don't understand how or why, but on impact, I passed out, slid out of my chair onto the floor. Seeing I was out cold, Dad threw the iced tea from his glass at my face to revive me. Although I was out for mere seconds, I had a clear vision I was at the Battle of New Orleans with Andrew Jackson.

Because of the pain in my eye and the concern about my blacking out, it was decided I should go to the hospital. As a youngster, I never thought about the embarrassment for my father to have to explain what happened. I was given some drops for my eye and told to wear an eye patch for a week. I became the pork chop pirate, and for a seventh grader, that was cool.

When my dad retired after twenty-two years of service in the Navy, we relocated to the city of Webster, Florida. This is the area where my mom grew up, and her mother still lived there on the old homestead.

We had always lived near the ocean as Dad was in the Navy. During the summer, we often went to the beach after Dad got home, and a quick supper was enjoyed. However, after moving to Webster, the quick afternoon beach runs were out of play. Then Dad heard about Shady Brook, more of a wayside park off Highway 301, but it had a swimming hole.

Shady Brook was small. It was a natural spring, its waters a cold, refreshing relief from the summer heat. On probably our second trip to swim and play, my younger brother was on my shoulders as we were having family fun. Suddenly I stepped backward and was way over my head. I could swim to save myself, but with my brother on my shoulders and him grabbing my head to hold on, I started to sink.

The next thing I felt was a strong push through the middle of my back, and I was being elevated. Breaking the surface of the water, I gasped for air and realized Dad had dived in, rescuing my brother and me. We never again had a family swim at Shady Brook.

Dad was still young after retiring from the Navy. He was continuously working to provide for our family, first as a carpenter, then as a manager in the local feed store, then working at the state prison close to home, eventually working in the local post office. While at the state prison, he coordinated sports activities, and our pickup softball team played there several times over the summer. A softball tournament was scheduled, and several prison teams were set to participate. Because of the number of visitors, some of the ground rules were changed. The biggest change was if a ball crosses the perimeter road, it was left alone; it was a ground rule double. Previously we just waved toward the guard towers and kept running to get the ball.

I was playing left field later in the day when a ball was driven deep, sailing over my head, bounced on the perimeter road, and rolled toward the fence. In full game mode, I charged across the road, waving my arm, going for the softball. Just feet from the prison fence, I reached the ball…then I heard people shouting. Looking up, I was between two guard towers, and guns from each were trained on me. I dropped the ball, hands up, and slowly backed away from the fence. Several inmates told me later not to be stupid; the guards don't play.

My dad had a tough life growing up. His mother passed away when he was twelve, and his father, when he was seventeen. He was a devout Christian, very active in church, serving the Lord. Dad loved our mother, and no one, especially us kids, was allowed to disrespect her. His devotion to her was a model for all of us to follow.

As children, we all knew Dad loved us; although, until later in life, there weren't a lot of hugs and I love yous. He would move heaven and earth to help his family.

The fall of 1979 found me married and attending the University of Florida. I was working with the sports department as a student athletic trainer, expanding on my previous two years with the Gators and time in the Baltimore Orioles farm system. More importantly, I was back in school, this time as a student applying myself.

As part of the training staff, I received a couple of tickets to football games. Now, to be honest not many Gator fans talk about going to a game in the '79 season the team finished the season 0–10–1. My dad joined me for the last home game of that season. It was an odd numbered year, so the final game was with Florida State. They were having a very good season undefeated and ranked fifth in the country.

Sitting in the stands with my dad just felt special that day. We watched the teams warm up, many fans were hopeful for a win, but knew it would take a miracle. Florida had worn blue and white uniforms for years, but the coaches wanted to ignite the players and the fans. So while the Gators warmed up, the managers laid out brand-new orange uniform tops. I had insight into what was happening and told my dad to be ready for a surprise.

As the PA announcer started the "Hhhhhere ccccccome the Gators!" intro, the orange-clad players charged onto the field, and the fans went wild. Sometime during that run onto the field, I felt this big arm wrap around me, and Dad said above the roar of the crowd, "I'm proud of you." It was spontaneous, but so real, I felt ten feet tall. I knew it wasn't a sporting moment; it was a life moment.

I still attend a lot of sporting events, first with my son, now with my son and grandsons. Nearly every time the stadium grows quiet and "The Star-Spangled Banner" is played or sung, I sense my dad's presence, and I'm encouraged to be a better father and grandfather.

I love you, Dad!

WHO DO YOU KNOW?

I find myself sitting outside the office of the dean for the College of Education at the University of Florida. I had a message given to me by a professor, saying the dean wanted to see me at my earliest convenience. My mind was racing as I sat outside the office and drifted back through my school history. Why was I here? What had I done? The dean's office, *really*?

As written in other chapters, with my father being in the service our family moved around the country. Nowhere was that more evident than in my education. When I entered South Sumter High School for the ninth grade, it was the ninth different school I had attended.

Starting with an uneventful kindergarten year in San Diego, we were living in Florida for the first grade, Center Hill Elementary. It was a small school. The first and second grade students shared the same classroom and teacher. I've been blessed to be fairly ambidextrous; I colored and drew with both hands. However, writing was best done left-handed. This was unacceptable to my teacher; she began forcing me to write right-handed. This continued until my mother visited the school more than once.

It also marked the first time I crossed the red line and got into double trouble. My sister was in the second grade; so when I got paddled at school for kissing girls, she promptly informed Momma after we got home. Yes, I got paddled again.

The highlight of that year had to be winning the Halloween costume contest. Dressed as a hobo with patches sewn on by Mom, carrying a handkerchief pouch on a stick over my shoulder. We walked through downtown as the city turned out to cheer us. Among them was my uncle Gary, who worked at the post office. He always threatened to put me in the postal bag he hung daily for the train and ship me to my dad, stationed in New York.

The second grade found me on Long Island, but the third grade showed some stability as we would live in Virginia Beach for more than five years. Attending Kempsville Elementary, we were in the library when I felt sick. The librarian called the office. The principal came in, said I looked fine, but the words were not fully out of his mouth when I vomited onto his pants and shoes. He quickly left, and I went to the sick room.

I was not the best student. Seems I always got notes saying, "Ronald does not apply himself," not the best message in a military household. I flew a lot of flags (Fs) along with Ds. I did just enough to get the next grade. Mom kept all my old report cards, putting them in a memoir album of my youth. I've never shown them to my children. They may disappear one day.

One thing that may have affected my schooling was health. I struggled with asthma when I was a child. Outdoor activities were restricted; I missed a lot of school days. However, I outgrew asthma. School attendance became a source of pride, and from the seventh grade through the twelfth, I had Perfect Attendance each year.

In November of the eighth grade, Dad retired from the Navy. We relocated to home, Webster, Florida. The best thing that could have happened to young Ronald… From day one, things were different. I was once again in a small school, when the bell rang the entire eighth grade walked from English next door to history class. Before the end of the year, I was on the Honor Roll and never looked back. Many members of the Webster Junior High class of 1968 became lifelong friends and have had positive impacts in the world. I still cherish my class ring.

High school flew by. I had great teachers, encouragers like Danny McCoy, Coach Dale Swain, Sam Harris. I did get paddled once again, talking in phys ed—not the smartest of moves, the wooden paddle pops for real when you're wearing gym shorts. Too small to play sports, but loving sports, I became an athletic trainer. This allowed me to be actively involved with football, basketball, and track. My grades remained good, I graduated with honors, joining eighty-three students to make up the Class of 1972.

I received a scholarship to Miami-Dade Junior College North to attend school and participate in their sports program as an athletic trainer. I called numerous times to confirm my acceptance, always asking for Scott Hall. Hanging up on some occasions because I couldn't reach him. Numerous letters said to call Scott Hall, room 123, and the phone number. On the first day of registration, I found myself inside a building that was the hub of activity—Scott Hall.

There were more people standing in line to sign-up for classes than in my whole hometown of Webster. I was bewildered, but I soon learned athletics had privileges. The assistant basketball coach walked by, saw me in line, told me to come with him, he walked me through a side door to the front of a virtually empty room. He explained to the people at a table I was with the athletic department, and my registration was completed in a matter of moments.

Dave Lawson, the head athletic trainer for sports at Dade-North, became a mentor, teacher, and encourager. He was a steadying force during my two years. His impact on my future cannot be overlooked.

The fall of 1973 was hard as fuel shortages hit hard to everyone with a vehicle. Long lines and limitations on gallons allowed made obtaining gas nearly impossible. After a tough couple of days with no gas, my roommates devised a scheme. Taking a rubber hose, we went on a gas siphoning expedition. Only two of us knew how to siphon; I was one of the two. With three near-empty gas tanks late that night, we headed to parking lots. We collected a few gallons here and there, but then at an apartment building on Twenty-Seventh Avenue, we hit the jackpot. A big Cadillac donated over twenty gallons to our cause. The night was a success.

There is an old prophecy "Your sins will find you out." The next afternoon, I entered the training room following soccer practice, Doc Lawson was finishing up after baseball practice. Then he dropped the bomb: my cosiphoner had collapsed on the field during running drills. Rushed to the hospital, the flu was the story, but the ER staff correctly diagnosed he had obviously swallowed gas the night before. They said he'd be okay, but they were seeing the problem a lot because of the gas crisis. The siphoning trips ended immediately.

Living away from home for the first time and being around sports and athletes, my focus on studies slowly began to slip. I did graduate on schedule in the spring of 1974, but it was becoming obvious that sports and the sporting lifestyle were the focus of my life.

In the spring of 1974, thanks in large part to Dave Lawson and Dr. Demi Maneri, the highly respected head baseball coach at Miami-Dade North, I was hired by the Baltimore Orioles as athletic trainer. This full-time position allowed me to develop as an athletic trainer, live with professional athletes, and become more entrenched in the sporting lifestyle.

The University of Florida was on a quarter system for classes, which worked perfectly for me. I could work the minor league season and attend the university for two quarters. I was accepted into the College of Education and to work with the athletic department as a student athletic trainer. Once again, I was blessed with a great situation.

Chris Patrick was the head athletic trainer at the University of Florida. He was outstanding as an athletic trainer, but as I learned over my time there, he was an even better individual. Chris welcomed me, and I went to work right away. Classes got underway. I was able to eat my meals with the athletes in the Yon Hall dining room.

I lived off campus with Rick and Kenny, two friends from the class of '68 at Webster Junior High and High School. They were both excellent students and were also in the School of Education. They had taken many of the courses I was now in. They offered notes, old tests, books, and help. Life was good, or was it too good?

I had no problem attending class, but sports and easy living led to a total lack of focus on studying. As grades slipped, I didn't get the message; additionally, there were no letters from teachers to Mom and Dad. After two quarters, I was on "academic probation"; but no problem, I was headed back to minor league baseball.

After just three quarters, I was expelled from the university for poor academic performance. I got a wake-up call. Although I tried, no sports hierarchy could save me. For the first time in a long while, I had stepped in it, and all the stink was on me.

Embarrassed and ashamed of myself, I had to be honest with my family and friends. This proved to be the kick in the pants I earned and needed. I was forced to examine my life, realize I'd been living a somewhat privileged life, and that success earned is success appreciated.

Oh, my life changed, but the good Lord still had his hand on me. During the next minor league season, I was asked to work in the Venezuelan Winter League. For three years, I worked the Minor League season in Miami, had six weeks off, and flew to Venezuela for the winter baseball season. After returning to the states, I had several weeks free before spring training. This was an incredible time of learning, travel, and maturing.

After three years away from the university, becoming married, I realized the obvious, returning to school and completing my education was critical to my long-term interest. In the fall of 1979, I returned to the University of Florida.

I was greeted with open arms by the athletic training staff. Chris Patrick made a point to regularly follow up with me on my academic progress. Maybe I had matured some, maybe being married changed my focus, or maybe the encouragement of friends and family, but I tackled my classes and was doing quite well.

Why did the dean of the College of Education demand to see me? I sat outside of his office, watching the clock, perplexed, but nothing prepared me for what was about to happen.

I was invited to come into his office, directed to sit down, then after a long minute or more of silence and a hard stare, he spoke with a harsh tone.

"Who do you know?"

I sat with a blank stare.

Again, he said stronger and louder, "Who do you know?"

I stammered, "I don't know what you are talking about."

Leaning forward in his chair, elbows on his desk, staring a hole through me, he asked once again, "I want to know...who do you know? I personally wrote a letter to your file stating to *never* readmit you to the university and definitely not into the College of Education." After a long pause, he asked once again, "So, Mr. Hart, who do you know? How did you get back into this college?"

In total shock, I tried to explain I followed the normal admissions process. Furthermore, I was not the same student. I had matured, I was married, and I was doing quite well in my classes.

He just sat there, glaring, waiting for me to come clean with names and who was paid off. After a quiet moment, I added I fully intended to apply to the College of Health and would be changing my major before the spring semester.

Finally, a look of normalcy came to his face, as he indicated that would be a good decision and he was in full agreement. That ended the visit. No "Good luck," "Take care," or "Have a good day." He made it seem like this wasn't over yet.

The Rest of the Story

I did quite well with the second chance given me at the University of Florida; however, life had different plans. I was offered an opportunity to interview with the Miami Dolphins, already knowing their athletic training staff and team doctors I may have had an inside track. School was going so well, I declined.

We found out we were expecting, after family discussions and with the Florida Training staff, decision was made to leave the Baltimore Orioles. This would eliminate road trips and allow more family time. Additionally, I was on track to graduate in August and was having conversations about becoming a graduate assistant at another university to be paid and work on a master's degree.

My wife got very sick during the early stages of the pregnancy, was hospitalized, and because of ongoing problems, she returned to Miami to be with her doctors and family.

As medical bills began to come in, I was not earning a paycheck. Funds were scarce, so after the winter quarter, I left the university to be with my wife and find a job. I must point out Chris Patrick was very supportive and offered me room, board, and a job so I could still attend classes. My parents said they would assist also. However, I declined, saying it was best for my family if I returned to Miami.

Later that summer while pushing a UPS cart in downtown Miami, I had a discussion with a coach/recruiter for the Aguilas of the Venezuelan Winter League. He offered me a job at such good pay as athletic trainer that when I said no, a part of me fell off and slid into the sidewalk. I never worked as an athletic trainer again.

Our son was born in September, five days after I started a job where I would work the next *forty years*. Nine years later, after attending several years of night school, I graduated with a Bachelor of Science degree, majoring in Health Services from Florida Atlantic University. Proudly walking across the stage, a friend, not realizing I was graduating, yelled from the crowd, "Great job, Rocket!" aptly caping a long journey.

THAT EMBARRASSING MOMENT—ARE YOU SPEAKING TO ME?

Sports are in my blood, and although I was not an athlete, they have provided me with many opportunities including travel and employment. In the seventies, I had the good fortune to work in the Venezuelan Baseball Winter League for three seasons. They enjoy baseball and take their local team very seriously. Just look around the major leagues at the number of players from there.

I soon found myself loving the country and its people. The seventies were prosperous times in Venezuela, and as the part of a baseball team, I traveled to the league cities and then explored on my own or with teammates. Everywhere I went, the people were kind, generous, and proud of their country.

I'm starting down another rabbit hole…

The 1976–1977 season was my first and found me in the wonderful city of Maracaibo as athletic trainer for the Aguilas de Zulia. Maracaibo was a bustling rapidly growing city. Oil was the predominant industry in the area, but the citizens had their local markets and were very proud of their native Guita music. What an opportunity to grow not only as an athletic trainer, but also as a person, working within a different culture, with Venezuelan players and players from many major league organizations.

The home of the Aguilas was Luis Aparicio Stadium, and our team manager was Hall of Famer Luis Aparicio. Correction, the manager was Luis Aparicio *Junior*. The statue out front was of his father, and stadium was named for him because of his remarkable baseball skills.

Some things were different from the start. Instead of batboys to retrieve the hitter's bat, we had batmen. They were older, took a lot of pride in their work, and were ever ready. A second Aguila tradition was the use of Base Girls several times a game. These base girls were a group of three or four scantily clad young women who flowed through our dugout on their way to sweep off the bases, much to the enjoyment of the crowd as they posed and flirted with the players. Many of us in the dugout assisted them in and out, and over the course of the season, we got to know them by name and did our own flirting. Enough said...

I only spent one season with the Aguilas, but my time there was wonderful. I thoroughly enjoyed being immersed in the culture, the people, and our shared passion for baseball.

My second and third seasons were spent in the quaint city of Maracay, home of the Tigres de Aragua. It was a smaller city and just a two-hour car ride from Caracas. The team management arranged for the out-of-country players and staff to live at a country club just north of the city, not only having the open spaces of the golf course, but also a very large pool and patio area.

One of the most memorable moments of my life happened one night when the electric power went off for a couple of hours. I made it downstairs and out onto the patio area. It was a crystal-clear night, and the stars were glowing. I had learned there are many more stars visible in the Southern Hemisphere; but this night (while still north of the equator), players, families, and others stood in amazed silence. We were in awe of nature and the Creator... But back to my story.

A third major change in my Venezuelan career was I returned a married man. We enjoyed our time in Maracay. We met several local families; the team had also provided us with a car, so we were much more mobile.

We were having a good season, so to show appreciation to the players, the team arranged a family road trip. We would fly to Maracaibo for a weekend series. I was eager to show my wife the city I had embraced.

During my duties as tour guide around the city, we found ourselves strolling hand in hand along the large plaza in front of the basilica and just off the downtown waterfront. I was full of myself talking up the city and its people.

Suddenly, there was a loud voice—a loud feminine voice I recognized. A local taxi, a poor man's ride, with several attractive young women was slowing for a red light. The passengers were all waving and calling my name, rolling their *R*s "Rrronnie, Rrronnie!" Turning to look, I saw a well-endowed base girl and others leaning far out of the window, blowing kisses and waving.

Stunned and frozen, I couldn't reply. I believe I managed a small shush wave. I had nowhere to hide, but I did note we were no longer hand in hand. The light changed, and their vehicle moved on with them still waving...

What a way to start my first weekend away with my wife.

AN ANNIVERSARY
TO REMEMBER

Travel is wonderful! Ever since I was a child, my parents planted the seed to get out, see parks and historic sites near our home. Throughout my life, travel has brought great joy and memories to me and my family.

My work as an athletic trainer kept me very busy in season, but also provided time between seasons to get away. One of those opportunities coincided with our first wedding anniversary. My wife had wanted to visit Europe for many years, so it was decided we would head to Europe in September.

My wife fully embraced the planning, and as her excitement grew, it was soon shared with friends. They also got caught up in the fun of planning the adventure. After a few months, it was decided two of my wife's girlfriends would be traveling with us. We would fly into Luxembourg, rent a car, and the four of us would be sharing a Switzerland-focused journey. We would also include Germany, Austria, Italy, France, and even a night in Monaco.

We had our route highlighted on several maps (no GPS in those days). We only had a few nights prebooked, so we would drive, enjoy sites and places along the way, and then check out potential hotels for the night. Thankfully, the custom of the time was to inspect a room before agreeing to stay. That was its own adventure—a lot of hand signs, broken speech, and written money figures.

Stop, I'm starting down a rabbit hole, need to stay on track.

As mentioned earlier, Switzerland was the primary focus of the trip, and it didn't disappoint. It was beautiful, with snowcapped mountains, alpine lakes, and lush green meadows. It was spotlessly clean, and we felt very safe. I still remember the looks and pointed fingers as people realized *This guy is traveling with three women.*

We arrived in Zurich on the day of our anniversary. We had no special plans except for some quiet time that evening. We checked into what appeared to be a large old house that had been converted into a bed-and-breakfast. We were blessed with a large corner room with many windows with views of the city. One area of concern was the separation from the room next door. Along one wall was a door frame stuffed with an old mattress and covered with a curtain.

However, next to the door frame was a huge armoire. You could have stored a month's supply of clothes between its hanging area and large drawers. I tried to slide the armoire to block the area, but I couldn't begin to budge it.

That evening, we retired back to the room for a quiet night. We had secured a bottle of wine from a food cart earlier in the trip. I poured the wine, but it was so bitter it was undrinkable—so much for free anniversary wine. We talked for a while and went to bed. There was just enough light filtering through the windows to act as a nightlight.

Shortly afterward, we were both awakened; we looked at one another but were not certain why both of us awoke. As we rolled back over, we both heard a noise in the hallway, and we felt uneasy. Sitting up in bed, we listened; it sounded as if someone was turning door handles and coming up the hallway toward our room.

Then they were at our door. The handle turned, and the door just started to open when a heavily accented voice said "Aye pardon." The door slammed shut. I sprang out of bed and ensured our door was locked and secure.

As we sat there in bed on full alert, it seemed as if the person had entered the room adjoining ours. There were rustling noises coming from the room and talking in whispers; we agreed something was going on next door. Neither of us felt comfortable at all. She was holding a water glass, ready to throw if needed.

Suddenly, it happened. The curtain that was hanging in the blocked doorway began to move, and it looked as if a person was moving through it. Out of nowhere, I yelled to my wife, "Get the gun! I'm going to have to shoot somebody!"

The curtain went flat, the door in the adjoining room slammed shut, and someone could be heard running down the hallway. Without hesitation, I jumped up, grabbing the armoire, and slid it across the entryway, blocking the access.

Together in bed, we tried to recount what had just happened. We did conclude we were safe. However, after a minute or two, her attention turned to our friends traveling with us. Were they safe? Had they experienced any problems? We had to find out.

Getting dressed, we walked down the hall and around the corner to their room, half expecting to be confronted at any time. Knocking on their door, we were happy to hear they were sleeping soundly. We shared our experience and our concern for them, said goodnight, and got up to leave.

"No way!" was the response.

"Excuse me," I replied, "we need to go back to our room."

The balance of our first anniversary night passed sharing a room, three young women in bed, and me sleeping on the floor.

The Rest of the Story

To this point in my life, I've never owned a gun, much less traveled to Europe packing it. I truly believe the good Lord put those words in my mouth that night. "Thank You, Jesus," as my mother would've said.

QUE PASA?...OH NO, NO, NO

In the late seventies, I traveled to Cuba with my wife. Although her parents came to America in the early fifties, some of her family still lived outside of Havana. This would be the first time for her to meet her grandmother and other family members. We were looking forward to the trip.

I was in my midtwenties, but on arrival at the airport, it was as if we had stepped into a time machine back to the fifties. Nearly all the cars were models from the 1940s and 1950s. Large, heavy-duty, but built to last. I was soon to learn mechanics were highly valued and often manufactured needed replacement parts themselves.

We transferred to the Hotel National in downtown Havana. Once again, it was like an old movie set. Very little of the infrastructure had been updated since the "revolution." Life seemed to move a step slower, which was not a bad thing.

The next morning, we met family members and moved from the hotel to their homes. We would be staying at Grandmother's house for a few days. They were very happy to welcome us. Extended family and neighbors were excited, as was my wife. Nearly all the food was rationed (a concept I didn't yet understand), but everyone was pooling resources for our trip.

We were toured by car, visiting many sites around Havana. It was a beautiful old city; highlights were the National Capital Building, a stroll along the "Malecon" with the Castillo in the background. There were many old historical structures, and with all the old vehicles, you were transported back in time.

We also traveled east of the city to Varadero. The wide sweeping white sand beaches there are spectacular, providing a contrast to the clear blue waters of the Straits of Florida. There is no question; Varadero is one of the world's great beaches.

As nearly all visitors traveling to be with family in Cuba, we came bearing gifts, much-needed items for health and general wellbeing.

Anyone familiar with the baseball history in the Caribbean could tell you of the Sugar Kings and the great Cuban players. The people love the sport of baseball, starting with kids playing stickball to adults of all ages. Once again, I was to learn how much.

As a child growing up, when a wooden bat would break, it was all hands-on deck to save the bat. We would try finishing nails and tape to extend the life of the bat. In Cuba, because of the lack of bats, they took the rescue to a whole different level. It was almost a science project as bats were often broken and restored multiple times.

In the midseventies, aluminum bats had just started gaining popularity in America. They were cumbersome compared to modern aluminum bats, but they were rugged and rarely broke. In Cuba, most had never seen metal bats. When I pulled a couple of them out of our luggage, it was like Christmas morning.

Additionally, because of my connection with Minor League baseball, we brought over two dozen brand-new baseballs. The kids and adults were very excited. The balls were not passed around but hidden away and rationed out very slowly.

Two decades later, one of our nephews explained the baseballs meant so much to him, the family, and the neighborhood. The high-quality balls lasted much longer and provided fun for a long time. He literally said I couldn't ever understand the joy those balls brought.

It was a privilege to share with others and see they truly appreciated the items.

I'm starting down another rabbit hole, so let me get back to our trip.

On one of the last mornings of the trip, some of the relatives said they needed to go to Havana and asked me to come along. I said, "Why not? Let's go."

It wasn't long before we were driving back streets in the city. We turned into a large maintenance yard for city buses and vehicles. We parked in front of an open bay door, one of the men got out of the car and went inside to speak with a mechanic. After several minutes, he was back and said everything was good.

I was thinking that was uneventful, wondering where we were headed next. It didn't take long for me to have an answer. We drove out of the maintenance yard, made a right turn, and were slowly traveling along the outside wall of the maintenance yard. We got to a certain spot, pulled over, and parked. My relative got out, looked around, and was standing leaning against the wall. My gut was telling me to pay attention.

The wall around the maintenance yard was made of concrete blocks, probably ten feet tall, with barbed wire across the top. Suddenly, one of the blocks in the wall began to shift. It was slid out of place, leaving a gap in the wall. Then, several auto parts were passed through the hole. I was beside myself, scared, trying not to show it, or be obviously looking around. Then, just as smoothly, the concrete block was pushed back into place. The parts were bagged, everyone was back in the car, and we were on our way.

What's happening? Oh no, no, no... I thought. I'm in an authoritarian communist country, feeling like I'm being watched all the time, police are armed with assault weapons, and I'm riding with relatives who just stole auto parts. I'm the only one sweating. *Please wake me up! Is this really happening?*

We casually drove away toward the house. My head was on a swivel, looking in all directions. One of the guys tells me to relax, that there is nothing to worry about. For them, this was not a daily outing, but it was not out of the ordinary. This event was constantly on my mind; I didn't feel comfortable until our plane landed back in Miami.

After getting safely back to the house, we were able to go with relatives to a government "tourist" store and buy them some basic necessities. But not unexpectedly, prices were very high. Later, we said our goodbyes, and they took us back to our hotel as we had to fly home the next morning.

This brief trip was a real eye-opener. A beautiful country with kind, caring people, but to see people oppressed by their government, rationed groceries, empty shelves, not knowing who to fully trust, stuck in a time warp, makes you appreciate the freedoms we take for granted.

The Rest of the Story

Many of the relatives we met on our trip were able to relocate to the United States in the years after our trip. They worked hard and have enjoyed many of the advantages of living in a free country.

My wife's grandmother did travel to Miami on a short trip of her own, able to see and stay with her daughter. It was a special reunion. Sadly, she could not accept the freedoms she experienced. She was convinced it was all a show put on for her, a guest from Cuba.

The year 1978 seems like long ago, but the people of Cuba still struggle for basic needs we take for granted. We can't let our children and grandchildren ignore history and the impact communism has had on this island so near us.

THIS CAN'T BE MY ROOM

One of the best things about working in the Venezuelan Baseball Winter League was being able to travel to various parts of the country. The countryside is beautiful, with green rolling hills, long sandy beaches, and others lagoon-shaped with rocky outcrops protecting them.

The city of Caracas was not taking a back seat to the rural landscapes without an argument. In the seventies, it was a bustling, vibrant city. Most of the league games were at night, so when playing one of the two teams based in Caracas, there was ample time to stroll through the plazas with their fountains and monuments. The city was lush and green. If you wanted to see it from above, there was a gondola that transported you to the top of Mount Avila to overlook the entire metropolis. You could turn, looking north, and see the Caribbean coastline and its beaches. Another lift serviced that side of the mountain.

We are talking baseball, so when in Caracas, the question always was, "Leones or Tiburones?" noting the two home team mascots. So when I would say Aguilas—or later, Tigres—I would be waved off. As noted in other stories, the people of Venezuela were very friendly, helpful to a fault, and generous. In Caracas, it was no different.

The nightlife in Caracas was hot back in the day too. One of the favorite hangouts of athletes was a disco by the name of La Pelota. There was always action there, and it was normally full of beautiful people.

One evening after enjoying the disco for a while, I headed back to the team hotel. As was the norm, players and staff had shared rooms. I got to my room, unlocked the door, and saw several others were visiting with my roommate. I walked in and said hello, explained my early return, saying I was tired. Then I realized what I had walked into…

In my room was my roommate, a major league player, a second teammate also playing in the big leagues. Additionally, two members of the Harlem Globetrotters were introduced. However, the primary attraction was lines of cocaine laid out on a board ready to be snorted. Of course, I was invited to join the party.

I was stunned. I couldn't breathe and could hardly move. I wasn't totally naive; cocaine was a popular drug with those who could afford it, especially in my South Florida home base. But I was in a foreign country, trying to take a hard stand against drugs. The police were tough in Venezuela, and I'm in an ideal "Let's make an example" situation.

Ever since, I've questioned myself for not excusing myself, fleeing to the safety of the lobby. However, I turned down the offer, changed, crawled into bed, and began some of the sincerest prayers of my life. Between the prayers, I could hear conversation about the good quality of the local drug and how more could be secured before leaving the area.

Thankfully, the visit ended without any disruption, and so ended one of the most fearful nights of my life.

The Rest of the Story

The two major leaguers. One cleaned up his life and had a good career. The second had a brief "cup of coffee" in the show. The two Globetrotter players I never saw or heard from again.

NIGHTTIME
CONVERSATIONS

Sleeping has never been difficult for me. As a child, I was always tired following a day of bouncing around, just being a kid. As a young adult, just give me a place to relax, and I would drift away in a heartbeat. Riding buses in minor league baseball, even with the noise of the players, was no problem.

As I got older and my children started driving, there was an exception. When my son drives, I can sleep like a baby. However, when either of my daughters are behind the wheel, I'll try hard to relax, but one eye is always open.

This story is not about my ability to sleep; it's about what I did while I was sleeping. Somewhere along the line, I began expressing myself while in deep sleep. As best I could tell, when I was in my early twenties, I began talking in my sleep. It wasn't every night, but when I had something to say, it flowed freely.

My roommates thought I was pulling a prank. Often sitting up, using hand motions, nodding my head while I was chatting away. My conversations were clear, normally about recent events. On nights I went to bed early, if I began to speak, my roommates would gather in the room and watch.

One such night, I sat up, turned to the nightstand, and talked out a letter while writing it. There was no pen in my hand, but I proofed the letter, folded it, tucked it in an imaginary envelope, licked and sealed it. Placed it on the nightstand and went right back to sleep. They all had a good laugh.

What was causing me to do this? Was I frustrated, unloading thoughts in my sleep? Apparently, it wasn't dreams of wild crazy events or bucket list items. I would call people by name, recall events, or on occasion let them know what I thought.

All of this is fine when I was a single person without many cares, but when I got married, it was a whole different ballgame.

We were married in the fall, and just weeks later, we traveled to Venezuela for the start of the Winter League Baseball season. We were away from friends and family whom we could talk with, sharing concerns or just talking about being newly married. As the season got underway, I once again became a nighttime chatterbox. This created a tough situation for both of us.

During the Winter League season, foreign players and their families generally lived in the same hotel. We stayed at a large golf resort with a massive pool and one restaurant. We all became like an extended family, seeing one another throughout the day. When the team went on road trips, the wives would lean even more on the new relationships.

Many professional ballplayers were known as party animals. I could understand that among single players, but I soon realized that carried over to many married players also. Remember the old adage, "What happens on the road stays on the road."

Within days of returning from playing in other cities, I would invariably begin to relate details of player escapades. Whether it was women throwing themselves at the men, crazy happenings while drinking, or visits to houses of ill repute. I even told of myself and others skinny dipping at the beach late one night.

Being a gossip was not good, even if it was true. This habit had to stop; my wife connected daily with wives of players. While she knew of their husbands' unfaithfulness, I give her credit for never mentioning anything, but I got interrogated many mornings.

We had been married about four months when my night speeches took a different turn. My wife had become very quiet. Discussions were brief, just the necessities, and silence. I was in the doghouse and had no clue as to why. After a couple of days, the beans finally spilled.

I had another talking episode. I sat up, looked straight at my wife, began wagging my finger, and unloaded. It was as if I had things well-practiced. I started listing complaints I had with her. I held back nothing, then with my tirade complete, I lay back down, returning to a deep, satisfying sleep.

"Wow, I did what?" All the things I had said were true in my mind, but I hadn't brought them out for discussion and wouldn't have in that manner. It was a totally one-sided finger-pointing session.

It was probably a good thing we were in a foreign country, with very limited phone service, no texting, or internet to schedule a flight. We had to have a long conversation. Thankfully, we did.

That was the only time in either of my marriages I went on such a rant. Gradually, I stopped talking in my sleep. As I mature, hopefully, I won't start back, but if I do, maybe they'll just consider it the craziness of the old guy.

THANK YOU, DR. V

The year 1980 marked the beginning of a new decade. "New and Unexpected" may be the best description of the wild ride my family and I were just embarking on. However, it wouldn't peak until early 1981. Let's take a look at this significant time in my story.

January 1980 started with me being a senior at the University of Florida, living in married housing. I was a student but was also working with the athletic department as an athletic trainer. My wife was working as a secretary on campus. Life was rolling along, things were in order, and it was good.

Late January turned into a time of big decisions. School was going very well, and there were strong possibilities I could graduate in August. The Baltimore Orioles had extended another contract to me and were discussing the start of spring training. Florida's head athletic trainer was speaking with me about finishing school, then he would work with me on becoming a graduate assistant, not at Florida but at a quality program. Then, in the midst of all these possibilities, my wife added we were expecting.

While celebrating having a child in the coming months, my wife and I had to focus and make decisions on what was best for our family. Minor League Baseball involved travel, and as I moved up in the organization, it would involve more time away from home. I informed the Orioles I was turning down their offer, stepping away from baseball and a job I truly enjoyed.

We had a due date in September for the baby. In the interim, I needed to focus on my studies and preparing for a new arrival. I was able to register for the spring quarter, and classes fell in order. An August graduation was almost assured and only months away.

I continued to work with the athletic training department, and their focus was turning to spring football practice. More talks were had with the prospective university, with a start date of January 1981. My wife continued working, and we were excited about the new direction of our lives.

February was moving right along. My wife was showing a bump, but a bigger bump lay ahead.

My wife began experiencing a heavy dose of morning sickness, which escalated into hospital stays. She was feeling miserable, couldn't work, and after another hospital visit, we decided she should return to Miami, where she could be with her doctors and family.

As the winter quarter wound down, hospital bills began coming in. My work with the athletic department was not a paid job, although it did have benefits. We had some savings, but with my wife not feeling well, us still seeing doctors, the rent to be paid, and the spring quarter's cost looming, I needed to find a paying job. I had begun working at Disney World on weekends in December, but it was just part-time and too far to attempt full-time while attending school.

Although the athletic department offered assistance, as did my parents, I made the decision to leave school, return to Miami, get a real job, and be with my wife.

In short order, I was working in the distribution center of a large retail store, Jordan Marsh (similar to JCPenney). I further supplemented that by working weekends and holidays as a taxi driver.

I enjoyed working for White Cab out of North Miami Beach. I was able to talk with people riding in the taxi and did very well with tips. Two sidebar stories: I was driving the night of the Miami Riots in May. A call came across the radio from dispatch telling us *absolutely not to drive* in an area they defined. I hurried to a pay phone, calling dispatch, asking what's happening? My family lives in the restricted area. I called it quits for the night, headed home, was stopped by two police roadblocks but made it home. Everyone was safe at home.

Secondly, I was working a slow night on New Year's Day 1981. I picked up a couple from Oklahoma on Miami Beach wanting to go to the Orange Bowl game. I said, "Let's go," they were big Sooner fans. I got them to the stadium, asked them where they were sitting, bought a cheap ticket, parked the taxi, went to a great game with Florida State losing by just one point, then met the couple and drove them back to their hotel. They were happy, and I was too, with the generous tip.

I left Jordan Marsh to begin working with Tony Roma's, a rib restaurant that was opening their first standalone drive-through. I was brought on as an assistant manager. I did get to meet Tony Roma and sliced the tip of my thumb, requiring stitches, while cutting onions for their famous onion ring loaf.

I enjoyed my jobs, however, when UPS made me an offer as a driver, I couldn't turn down the money. Wow, my pay nearly doubled, I was able to park the taxi for a time. But as noted in other stories, I was let go on my final day of probation.

The summer was moving along, my wife was feeling much better, the baby was due in weeks. We were living with her parents. "Ron, you need to find a good job where you can advance and stay for a while." Meanwhile, I was driving a taxi full-time.

I applied for a management trainee position with Rinker Materials, a building materials company. I was hired in late September and assigned to the North Miami plant. It was a training position just as they said; the first few months were all grunt work. However, I had a job with future potential and decent benefits. The pay wasn't great, so I continued driving a taxi on weekends.

Five days into the job, I called into the office, Bud answered the phone. "Hey, Bud, good morning. I need to let you know I'm not coming in today."

"I understand," he said, cutting me off. Then he added, "They treat trainees like crap. The last guy only lasted one day. I'll let them know you've had enough!" as he started to hang up the phone.

"Bud!" I yelled. "Don't hang up! I'm at the hospital. My wife is having our baby. I need my job!"

"Oh," he stammered.

I told him I'd update them later in the day, and I hoped to be back tomorrow.

That was the start of forty years working with the company. I returned to the North Miami plant on the day of my fortieth anniversary, walked the yard, thinking it really hadn't changed very much. But it kicked off a good career.

I'm starting down another rabbit hole, so I'll stop.

A year of change had settled with the birth of my son. All the swirling seemed to be over through the holidays. My wife was doing well, my son was healthy, work was going much better, I was learning to dispatch trucks, and funds from taxi work were stabilizing a lot of concerns.

Early in the new year, I got a severe case of the flu. I didn't miss much work, but I was miserable for about ten days. The flu bug just seemed to hang around. Finally, I was able to say my health was back.

Moving into February, things began to change health-wise. It began very slowly. I started tripping over my feet, not frequently; but over the course of about ten days, it began to happen more often.

I didn't pay much attention to it until I started losing the grip in my hands. At work, I would lift items that weren't particularly heavy, and they would slide through my hands. Then, within a few days, when applying pressure to write on my dispatch sheet with a pencil, the pencil would just fall out of my fingers. Again, not each time I wrote, but it was happening.

I was sitting at the dispatch desk; my mind was racing as I suddenly tied my tripping to my loss of hand strength. What was going on? I didn't have any idea, but it wasn't right. That evening, my wife asked me to hold the baby for a minute. I froze, said no, giving an excuse. I was afraid of dropping my son.

The next morning, I called the office of the baseball team's doctor, who was also the team doctor for the Miami Dolphins, Dr. Charles Virgin. Because I had a past connection with his office, they told me to come in that afternoon, and they would work me in. I was the last patient of the day.

After a moment of pleasantries, the doctor asked what was going on. He told me to take off my work boots and walk across the room. "No," he quickly said, "walk straight and don't swing your legs." I couldn't do it. Unconsciously, I had been swinging my legs to make up for the drop feet I was experiencing. He checked my hands; there was minimal resistance when he pulled against my fingers. Then he checked my reflexes, elbows, hands, knees, and feet. He was very quiet. I had mentioned earlier about my bout with the flu, and he asked for more details. Then he told me to sit down, get my shoes on, and he was going to make a phone call.

He called a neurologist. After saying hello, he asked if he would wait for me. I was a friend— "Please do him a favor"—and Dr. Virgin asked him to see me this afternoon. Then he used a big word I didn't know, *Guillain-Barré*.

I had known Dr. Virgin for several years but never like this. He looked me straight in the eye, saying, "The neurologist is waiting for you. Go directly to his office. He's going to put you in the bleeping hospital. Expect it and *don't* delay or question it. Go, he's waiting for you and good luck." My head was spinning.

Once in the office, the doctor had me strip down to my underwear. I did the walk, the reflexes, the hand grip. Then the doctor took a large safety pin, opened it wide, told me to look up and close my eyes. "I'm going to touch your feet and legs. Tell me if you feel sharp or dull."

"Okay," I replied, then, "Dull, dull, dull, dull, dull, dull!"

He said, "*Okay*, done."

Thinking I had passed the test, I looked down at my legs. Many large X-shaped scratches were on my legs, several were bleeding, and I'm saying "Dull!" *What is going on?* The doctor told me to get dressed. He added I was blessed to see Dr. Virgin. He thought I may indeed have Guillain-Barré, but tests would have to be done. I did need to go into the hospital immediately. Yes, I could go home to see my wife, take a shower, but then report to the emergency room. He would call in my admission.

Guillain-Barré syndrome is a rare disorder that causes your body's immune system to attack your nerves. It leads to muscle weakness or paralysis, sometimes both. Additionally, it can progress until it affects the respiratory system. The good news was most people fully recover, but it may take a few years.

Once admitted, I wasn't in the intensive care unit but was closely watched. I learned I was the first new case at the hospital in more than a year. I needed to learn about the syndrome and how it's cured. I was a brand-new dad and honestly, very scared. All kinds of thoughts run through your mind when you're confined to a hospital bed. Would I be able to carry my son, would we play catch, or stroll on the beach? I asked family, friends, and pastor to pray for me. I needed help and couldn't do it myself. I needed a miracle.

After a few days, my condition stabilized, meaning the muscle weakness and loss of feeling wasn't expanding, pleasing the doctors. The staff wanted me to be encouraged, so a joint physical therapy session was scheduled so I could meet a young lady, eighteen or nineteen, who had been hospitalized with Guillain-Barré for well over a year.

They had me lying on a mat when she was brought into the room, still confined to her wheelchair and with braces on her legs. I sat up unassisted, we talked for just a moment, when she demanded to leave, very upset, saying repeatedly through tears, "I don't have the same condition he has, look at him, and then look at me." Everyone was stunned, and the therapists were scrambling.

I later learned she had been very near death and on a ventilator for several months. She had fought valiantly to recover to her current state and wanted no comparison to me, a healthy-looking person. I believe she was correct.

Later that day, back in my hospital bed, thinking about the meeting, I was encouraged. I saw where the syndrome could have taken me. However, Dr. Virgin got me diagnosed, secured expert care, and many people were praying. With the disease in slow remission, I had been blessed. Indeed, I had my miracle.

I had a loving family, a good job, let the decade roll. What's next!

The Rest of the Story

In a matter of weeks, I was fully recovered. However, I still read precautions before taking some meds and vaccines, some say not to take if you've had Guillain-Barré.

The good Lord watched over me and put His healing touch on me. The Sunday after being discharged, I walked slowly down the aisle at church, still swinging my legs some, to give a testimony of His goodness. Indeed!

UNEXPECTED BLESSINGS

My life has been filled with unexpected blessings. So many times when it seemed I was in a jam or just needing reassurance, blessings arrived, reminding me that the good Lord is in charge and that there are a lot of good people in this world.

Many blessings we receive, we may not even realize in the moment, but we say "Wow!" after thinking about it later. Many of the chapters in this narrative are recaps of blessings. The following are special and stand apart from the routine.

You Could Use a Hug

A couple of years ago, I took a fall trip driving from South Florida as far west as Nevada and Arizona. I started off excited for the adventure that surely lay ahead. I took a long drive the first day, finally stopping in a rest area to sleep.

The next day, I arrived in Arkansas. I visited Petit Jean State Park, a beautiful park with mountain views, river overlooks, and hiking trails. Most of all, I wanted to see Cedar Falls. Located in a large bowl, water cascades ninety-five feet down the rocky face into a circular pool and with fall color, it's spectacular. I was getting amped up.

However, the waterfall was gone, just a wet spot on the rock face. At the lodge, the rangers said a prolonged drought had dried up the waterfall for the first time in many years. Waterfalls are one of three things I truly enjoy taking pictures of, and this was to be a trip highlight. Disappointed and tired from some light hiking, I pushed on.

On the plus side, because I didn't spend a lot of time hiking to and shooting pictures of the waterfall, I had plenty of time to head to Eureka Springs.

Eureka Springs is a scenic area with historic homes, hotels, and downtown; along with old churches (also on my photography checklist).

Checking my map and GPS, both pointed me to the Scenic Pig Tail Highway, only sixty-seven miles to Eureka Springs. This was great news because my original plan had me backtracking to visit tomorrow. Off I went... Have you ever seen a pig's tail? It's just a short series of spirals. What the map and GPS failed to tell me was there are 571 curves on the scenic highway... Oh my... I couldn't begin to enjoy any scenery, my eyes had to be focused on the road. Low speed and turn after turn had me suffering from road rage.

Finally, arriving in Eureka Springs, it didn't disappoint. What a gorgeous town, the only problem was the sun would be setting soon. I was rushing to take pictures, but Thorncrown Chapel was just outside of town. This large, beautiful church built on a hillside surrounded by trees has huge glass walls and windows to experience nature as you worship. It was a must-take photo, there's the entrance, what? A barricade across the roadway with a sign "Closed for Private Event." I couldn't see anything because of the hillside.

Suddenly, I was exhausted, disappointed, and very frustrated. My hotel was still at least an hour away. I was also hungry; I had passed a busy diner a couple of times in my jaunts around town. Driving back into town, I decided to stop, try to relax, and have a good meal.

After being seated, I realized I must look rough. Second day in these clothes, short night's sleep in the truck, only fast food for two days. I ordered a fried catfish basket, then headed to the bathroom to wash my hands, face, and comb my hair. Feeling better, I returned to my seat. The waitress laughed when I said I thought the "pig tail" was a shortcut. The iced tea tasted wonderful, and I had several glasses.

The waitress asked several times to be sure I didn't want dessert. After my repeated no and another glass of tea, I asked for the check.

She informed me I had no check; a young couple sitting near me, now long gone, had paid my tab and tip.

"Excuse me! Tell me again!"

"They paid for your meal."

Wow, I looked around, but she assured me they had left the restaurant. I thanked her, added to the tip, and headed out.

Only now was I feeling completely refreshed and trying to comprehend what had just happened. As I walked to my truck, I don't think my feet hit the ground. Sitting there in the dark, I prayed aloud, giving thanks.

The drive to the hotel was over in a flash, as I couldn't believe what had just happened. I had a great night's sleep, woke up on Sunday morning, and attended a wonderful worship service. Thank You, Jesus, for a much-needed hug.

The Rest of the Story

While I was sharing with everyone, I knew about how I had been blessed, a week later I was in Tony Roma's Restaurant in Las Vegas having dinner. I remember telling my waitress I had met Tony Roma while working as an assistant manager at his second restaurant in Miami.

I had been hiking throughout the day in Valley of Fire State Park. What an amazing park, an hour drive east of the city. Once again, I was tired, but I had showered, cleaned up, and was thinking about this rib dinner.

When I asked my waitress for my check, she told me two women at a nearby table had paid for my meal and tip. Of course, they had exited, once again I was left speechless.

Then a still small voice spoke to me saying, "If I did it once, why don't you believe I could do it a second time?" I walked back to my hotel grateful and humble.

A Sporting Gift

I've written a lot about how sports have been a big part of my life. They provided me with an education, livelihood, and entertainment. When I became a single parent when my son was three, it was no surprise that once again sports became a focus of things we could do together.

It seemed like our weekly adventure was to the park to run, play, slide, throw a ball, or shoot baskets. Normally, this was followed by a visit to McDonald's for a "Happy Meal." The truth be told, I was very appreciative of those inexpensive "Happy Meals." Many nights my son ate while I watched, not having money for a meal of my own.

The University of Miami won the College Football Championship in 1983. I attended some of the home games and got the idea to purchase season tickets for the 1984 season. The hope was that my son and I could go to the Orange Bowl, tailgate, spend the day together, and enjoy a college football game.

It was one of the best decisions of my life. The Hurricanes were playing great football, and we looked forward to each game. In the early days, it seemed my son always wanted a bathroom break at those critical moments and would spend most of the second half asleep on my lap. Watching the Canes was contrary to my Florida Gator roots, but we were having a great time together.

My son soon turned into a Miami Hurricane fanatic; he was all Canes all the time. This was never more evident than a few years later when we visited the University of Florida. We visited some of the athletic trainers, walked through the football locker room, and had the opportunity to walk out onto Florida Field. I was reminiscing, telling him how I ran out on the field with the team before the game while the fans went crazy. Interrupting my story, he got my attention and asked if he could pee on the field. *What?* I was a Gator dad failure.

In the early nineties, things became very tough for me financially. I needed to give up our season tickets, and this was going to crush my son and end a special father/son activity we enjoyed.

My family was active in our church. I taught Sunday School and worked with the youth; I had remarried, and my wife was in the choir and a gifted soloist. My son participated in activities and had several good friends.

A couple of men from the church met with me and said they wanted to pay for my season tickets for the upcoming season. I was stunned, thankful, and very happy. My mind went back to my days as a youth when a man in the church paid for me to attend summer camp. Wow... my season tickets paid in full. Once again, very blessed.

The Rest of the Story

This fall will be my fortieth as a season ticket holder with the Miami Hurricanes. It's been an amazing run. We've enjoyed incredible times, now I attend the games with my son and grandsons. Tailgating is wonderful and my son gets to shuttle the boys to the bathroom. This all happens because of an unexpected blessing I'm still grateful for.

"I Feel Good"

You never know when those unexpected blessings will occur. I am guilty of not always fully appreciating them in the moment. However, looking back, I just said, "*Wow, wow, wow!*"

In the seventies, I was working summers with the Baltimore Orioles farm team in Miami. It was arguably the best job I ever had. Going to the ballpark every day, prepping for the players to arrive, treating injuries, completing paperwork, then going down through the tunnel to watch the baseball game. If no one got banged up, it was clean up, shower, and head to the house. Repeat the next day.

That outline is a little simplistic, but working with great athletes, watching them strive to improve and reach their goal of the major leagues, was fun and very rewarding. My career was bookended by Hall of Famers Eddie Murray in 1974 and Cal Ripken Junior in 1979, and numerous others who achieved their dream of playing in the big leagues.

As an athletic trainer in the minor leagues, my job entailed a lot more than just watching ballgames. I worked closely with the team manager and the club's administration. The ball club's manager changed several times over the time span, but fortunately, the main office was headed by Sonny Hirsch most of my tenure. Sonny was a Miami sports icon, radio host, voice of the Hurricanes, and a passionate baseball advocate.

The team played home games at Miami Stadium, a great venue for baseball. For a minor league team, it was a huge ballpark with a large arched overhanging roof. The stadium was also the spring training home of the Orioles for many years.

Once the season was over or the team was out of town, the stadium hosted a lot of events. The shape of the ballpark made it ideal for concerts and a lot of them were held there. The agents and promoters coordinated the events with the team management and the City of Miami.

I was introduced to a young lady one afternoon by her cousin, who worked in the team office. As time passed, we fell in love and decided to get married. The team office staff, Sonny, and others were a tremendous help, from knowing jewelers to arranging a rental car for our honeymoon.

The day before our wedding, I picked up the rental car for our honeymoon, and it was beautiful. I drove over to the ballpark to say thanks and share my growing excitement. I went in and was immediately called to the back office. Sonny was there with a local promoter and a black gentleman who looked familiar, but I didn't know. I was then introduced to James Brown, "the Godfather of Soul."

After a couple of minutes of me stammering, I started talking about the wedding plans and thanking them. About the time I started to leave, James Brown reached into his pocket, pulling out a wad of bills. He peeled off a $100 bill, handing it to me, wishing me good luck.

I was blown away, not only by meeting him but his generosity. As I was leaving the front office, I yelled, "*I feel good*!" and could hear their laughter in the background.

These are just a few of the amazing, unexpected blessings I've received.

HELP FOR THE MAN DRESSED IN BLACK

In the early eighties, I became a basketball referee. Much of this is written about in other chapters. However, to start this story, let me say it was a big assist to my family as we were getting on our feet. Also, note this was the era before cell phones.

As a young official, I officiated nothing but junior varsity games, and most were at smaller private schools. Junior varsity games were played before the varsity teams squared off. I was able to change into my officiating uniform at work and drive directly to the school, getting there on time. It was to be this night.

We were living with our in-laws, and I had driven my father-in-law's car to work. After changing, I got into his Chrysler New Yorker and headed to Miami Christian High School. Just as I exited the expressway onto Eighty-Seventh Ave, I heard and felt the signs of a flat tire. It was just getting dark. I found a grassy spot and stepped out to see what was happening.

Indeed, I had a flat tire. I started to get ready to change it. The spare was also flat. *"Really!"* I yelled aloud. Here I am alongside a busy roadway, it's dark, and I'm dressed in all black—shoes, socks, pants, and jacket. I get the spare out of the trunk and prepare to roll it down the avenue, hopefully to somewhere they can repair it.

I had rolled the tire less than twenty yards when a man pulled up asking if I needed help. "Yes," I said. He opened his trunk, I tossed in the spare tire. We headed south; he asked where to, I had no idea. He simply said, "Okay, let's find something." After a couple of miles, there was a tire store, yes, things were looking up.

I got the tire, rolled it into an open bay, but was promptly told, "We are closing, nothing else tonight." I rolled the tire back to the car, explained to the man, and he said, "Wait here." He went into the shop, came right back out telling me to bring the tire.

After a quick patch, we were on our way back to the car. I should be at the gym already. The teams can play with only one referee, but it's tough for everyone. However, my tire is repaired. Back at the car, the gentleman tells me to stay back as he expertly changes the tire in the light of his headlights.

I ask if I could pay him, but he refused any payment. He added he would follow me toward the gym to be sure I got there. I am speechless, thankful, and suddenly anxious to get to the school.

As I drove toward the school, his car is right behind me until the final turn. I keep looking but don't see him again, and I'm at the school. I hustle toward the gym, fully expecting questions and dirty looks. I hear a game ongoing, but wait, that's not my scheduled game. Oh no, what's happening? Am I in the right place?

The bus bringing the girl's teams was delayed and was well over an hour late. I located my partner for our game, and the teams were ready to hit the floor once this game finished. I sat there, stunned, trying to get my head around what had just happened. Grateful to be on time for my game, but really, how do I explain this?

Looking back, there was no explaining necessary, only a testimony of how I was blessed and watched over from start to finish. What a night!

ARE YOU TONIGHT'S UMPIRE?

I've mentioned in other stories how much I enjoyed sports, which led me into officiating basketball. After several seasons, it was mentioned in a basketball official's meeting that the school system was in real need of baseball umpires. Officiating was really helping to make ends meet, providing exercise, and enjoyment. Now that I was becoming a single parent a second sports season seemed to make perfect sense.

I loved baseball. I'd played, worked with it, knew the rules, so why not be an umpire? I attended the clinics learning the finer points. Did better on the rules testing than nearly all my basketball exams. I bought all the needed gear. This was my sport; I was a natural.

Hi, How Are You Doing?

In high school games, I worked the bases. I needed to get practice before calling balls and strikes at a high school level. The best place to learn was in youth league games, and South Florida had leagues everywhere. It wasn't long before I was behind the plate and learning.

It soon became apparent that *learning* was one thing I needed to do. All those years of me yelling at umpires did nothing to make the art of calling strikes easier.

One evening, I had flipped a coin with my partner; I was to be behind the plate. The game was off to a good start, with a couple of quick innings. In youth leagues, pitchers are limited on the number of pitches they can throw. The second set of pitchers came in and the wheels came off the wagon. They were struggling to throw the ball across the plate.

As an umpire, you widen the strike zone, trying to find a strike, encouraging the pitcher, and hopefully getting the batters to swing. Achieving this balance can bring frustration from caring parents and fans. They started with, "Let's go, Blue!" "Punch a hole in that mask!" "Do you need my glasses?" Oh, it was often worse.

As the pitchers struggled, the crowd grew louder, but I was recognizing a set of voices. After another change of pitchers, the tone eased. But still, it seemed one couple was having issues with the home plate umpire. Just constant nagging! Suddenly, it hit me how I knew these voices. They were members of the class I taught at church.

At the end of the inning, I walked back to the fence, paused, took my mask off, and said hello, calling each of them by name. Their mouths fell open, and they stammered to say hello. After a brief conversation, the next inning started; it was so much quieter.

They did miss a class or two but were soon back and active. We never discussed umpiring again, but I never saw them at a ballgame either.

The Catcher Did What?

Youth baseball is great. Players have fun running the bases, catching that high fly ball, or getting their first hit. Parents exhort their children and cheer to the point of embarrassment when they make a play or get a big hit. Baseball is special, and the umpire shouldn't get in the way of the fun.

I was calling a game for kids sixteen and under. At this age, only the best are still playing. Many are on their high school team or trying to impress their school's coaches. This results in a well-played game, more innings completed, and less noise from the stands.

However, I was the exception and was having a rougher game than usual with the balls crossing the plate. I was never able to hit curveballs or sliders, and this night I wasn't seeing fastballs well either. The complaints were coming from each dugout, the catchers, and pitchers, in addition to the stands.

We made it to the later innings with the home team down by a few runs. I was becoming the scapegoat, not the team looking at their own shortcomings. When we got to the last inning, the first batter stepped into the batter's box. Then it happened…

The pitcher looked in, got the sign for the pitch, completed his wind-up, then as he released the ball, *the catcher fell over*! Yes, he just fell on his side. Meanwhile, a fastball, the hardest thrown all day, was coming straight at me. My concern was that the batter would foul the ball back, but I did have my gear on. Thank goodness there was no swing, and the ball bounced off my chest. The smirk on the catcher's face confirmed my gut feeling, this was not an accident.

I yelled "*Time out!*" and headed to the home team's dugout. The coach met me halfway. Before I could even get started, he was telling me the pitch was to be a curveball and the catcher was trying to block it. Right, coach, I don't think so.

Long story short… I instructed him to return to the dugout and not breathe until the game was over. Also, I'd be doing a full report for the league's commissioner.

You Seem to Be Struggling

In my second year of umpiring high school baseball, I was assigned to call a game at Southridge High School, working the bases. Southridge was one of the top baseball teams in Miami-Dade County. Upon arrival at the school, I recognized and spoke with several pro scouts I knew from my days with the Orioles. Yep, it was an important game for the teams in the standings and the players trying to impress scouts from colleges and professional teams.

The game got off to a good start, with a few quick innings, and things were rolling along. Finally, there were some base runners; each team had scored, but it was a close game. Late in the game, Southridge got their leadoff batter on at first. The third base coach gave the signs, and a steal of second base was set.

The runner got his lead off first, the pitcher wound up, and threw a fastball to the plate. The runner was off and running; the catcher bounced out of his crouch, letting the ball fly toward second base. The shortstop was covering the bag, the runner slid, and the tag was made. It was a close play, so all attention quickly shifted to me, the base umpire. What was the call?

I moved, getting in the best position to see and make the correct call. I took a long look, then swung my hands wide open, indicating the runner was safe. I stayed with the action, as we're taught to do. When the runner stood, stepped off the base, and was immediately tagged by the shortstop, I signaled and yelled out.

As the runner headed to his dugout, his coach was fired up and questioning why he got off the base. He responded, "He called me out!" to which the coach replied, swinging his hands open, "No, he said you were safe!" The runner shook his head, not sure what happened, but his teammates were telling him he was called safe.

As I moved to reposition myself behind first base, the second baseman told me, "Hey, you waved safe but yelled out!" I took a double-take. "What?" and he said with a laugh in his voice, "Yes, you did!"

I don't remember which team won that night, but it watered the planted thought that maybe I wasn't cut out to be a baseball umpire. As I was leaving the field after the game, one of the scouts I knew well said goodnight and added, "You seem to be struggling as an umpire."

The Rest of the Story

That was my final season as an umpire, at any level. I packed my gear, put it in the attic, and it's not been touched for over thirty years. I've often questioned how it was I couldn't succeed umpiring a game I loved. Was it my eyes or long hours at work before calling a game? Whatever it was, I rarely yell at umpires nowadays be it at my grandsons' youth league games or at a Miami Marlin's game. Maybe, I wasn't a natural.

TRAFFIC STOPS AND COURT VISITS

I am not a perfect driver; in no way do I want to say I didn't deserve to be ticketed on occasion when driving. However, there have been times when tickets were issued, and I had to scratch my head saying no way it was deserved. In this chapter are recaps of both.

Mr. Hart, Are You Listening to Me?

When I returned to Miami for my second year of college, I had a car. My uncle Charles did part-time work with a used car dealer. He was able to assess used cars and became a source of first cars for our family.

I purchased a beige 1964 Plymouth Belvedere for $500. The car had low mileage, was in great condition, and had a spotless interior. It was an excellent choice for being a first car.

I stopped for a red light on Northwest Thirty-Second Avenue on the west side of Miami-Dade College North. While stopped at the light, I saw a police car parked on the median no more than forty yards ahead of me. The light changed, I continued down the avenue, and noticed the policeman pull in behind me and then on came the lights. I had never been pulled over but found a wide area and stopped the car.

The officer said I drove through the light at forty-four miles per hour, and the speed limit is thirty miles per hour. I said, "I was stopped at the light and saw him parked on the median. There was no way I could have been speeding." The officer was very short and simply said, "He would see me in court, if I had any questions." I couldn't believe it, so I took his advice and scheduled a court date.

Going into a courtroom for the first time was intimidating. The judge was up front, policemen sitting together in one area, and regular folks, a few with attorneys, scattered around the room. I quickly realized it was also informal to a degree. Names were called, the policeman would explain why the ticket was given, the driver gave their reason for protesting the ticket. The judge would ask questions for clarity, followed by a pronouncement of judgment, points assessed, fine, and court cost to be paid. I just had to be confident in telling my story.

This day, many people were being told the ticket stood. Their excuses were just that, and the judge didn't want to hear them. She didn't hesitate to point out the fallacies in their story, however, she listened well and would fault the officer also.

Finally, my full name was read, my knees were weak as I strode to the front and stood near the policeman who stated his case. The judge then asked for the calibration certificate for the instrument used to measure my speed.

She frowned at the officer, saying, "Are you aware this document is out of date?"

He responded, "Yes ma'am, I didn't realize at the time of the incident, but it is."

The judge gave him an angry "Why are you wasting my time?" look. "Case dismissed!" she said loudly.

Turning to me, she said, "You are free to go. Drive safe." I hadn't given my defense, so I started explaining what happened. The judge cut me off, "Mr. Hart, are you listening to me? The case is dismissed!" I was nervous, wired, and continued to exonerate myself. "Mr. Hart, stop! The case against you is dropped, unless you want to reschedule a hearing, *you need to go!*"

Finally, with snickers of laughter in the courtroom, it hit me. I had won my case. I said thank you, headed out, as the judge just smiled and shook her head.

Yes, I Said It

Teaching my daughters to drive was no easy task. One was eager to learn, while the other was apprehensive. They both had the same first car, a mid-nineties Buick LeSabre, which was given to them by their grandmother. It was a great first car: big, full-size, four-door that offered plenty of protection, easing my dad concerns as they developed their driving skills.

There were some industrial warehouse parks being developed nearby, which made great training grounds on weekends. While my patience was tested, once committed to learning, they both did very well.

The Buick was nicknamed *The Boat*, and it was happily driven to high school, activities, and work. The car would eventually make it to the University of Florida and Savannah College of Art and Design. It wasn't the prettiest car in the parking lot, but it may have been the most appreciated.

The Boat also offered life lessons, but what happens when those clash?

As with all vehicles, *The Boat* required regular maintenance. I tried to teach my daughters the importance of taking care of your car so it would take care of you. A time came when the car needed its brakes worked on. I had a friend who could do it for me at a much-reduced cost. I set a time to drop it off at his home.

Well, my timing was not my daughter's. She needed to be at work by five o'clock, and a lot of factors would have to fall into place for this to happen. She would have to get home from school, change for work, and grab a snack. I would have to leave work early, get home, the two of us drive over to my buddy's house dropping off the car, and then drive her to work.

From first mention, she was against the plan. "Dad, it won't work. There is not enough time, you know it, you are going to make me late to work."

"Relax, be ready, and we'll make it happen," I replied.

"Dad, I can't be late to work," she insisted. "You've preached to me all my life about not being late to work. When was the last time you were late to work?"

She was probably right. "That's it! Let's go, we must get the maintenance done."

I drove to my friend's house; we were making good time. The signal lights were green one after another, we had a chance for this to work. On arrival at Mr. Vince's, she was in my truck in a flash, ready to go. However, I had to talk, after all, he was doing us a favor.

As I climbed back into my truck, "We are going to be late for sure," she said.

"If we go the back way, we will be okay," I said as she rolled her eyes. Of course, I knew she was correct, so I increased my speed.

We were heading west on Taft Street, making great time, when it happened. A motorcycle policeman stepped into the roadway, waving for me to stop. A *speed trap*! I was not happy. My daughter literally gave a karma clap, telling me without saying anything, "Justice, justice, justice!"

I lowered my window as the officer approached the truck. "Sir, you were doing fifty miles per hour in a posted thirty-five miles per hour—"

Frustration got the best of me. I barked cutting off his words *"Are you kidding me!"*

His jaw fell open, my daughter cringed, I realized what had happened, "I am sorry sir, I've never had a ticket and I snapped."

He still had a look of disbelief on his face, "Give me your license, registration, and insurance." Taking them, he walked back to his motorcycle.

My daughter was still in shock, "I can't believe you said that."

I responded, "Yeah, I don't know where that came from."

After a couple of minutes, nobody was mentioning being late for work, the officer walked back to our truck, cards, and a paper waving. "I checked back as far as I could, you are right. I saw no tickets on your record." Then he added, "So I'm *not* giving you one today, just a warning. Drive safe, and I don't want to pull you over again."

I thanked the policeman, assured him I'd be driving safe. We drove away in silence, my mind still racing, because of what I had said. My daughter looked to be feeling better but was still a little grumpy with me.

Arriving late to her job at the mall, I asked if she wanted me to go in, speak to her supervisor, taking the blame. "No, thanks, Dad. You've done enough already."

The Rest of the Story

The brake shoes got changed on *The Boat*. All three of my children have a strong work ethic and I'm grateful for that.

I was back in court on another occasion, had taken several pictures of the area where I was ticketed. The judge agreed with me.

On Thanksgiving driving back from my mother's, I got pulled over for speeding, started talking about other things with the officer, he wished me and my youngest daughter a safe ride home.

Oh, there were other opportunities for tickets too. As I get older, I find myself driving slower, life is still going to occur, don't rush it. I encourage everyone to follow the speed limit and respect our traffic officers.

THE UNEXPECTED WHEN DRIVING

I'm sure anyone who drives has had close calls and blessings. People assisting me to change a tire or giving me a few gallons of gas when I ran out have happened on more than one occasion. The following stories are unique to my fifty years of driving.

Surely, You Speak Spanish?

In other parts of my story, I've written about time spent in Venezuela. It was enjoyable, and the country holds a special place in my heart. We had a couple of days away from baseball, so we planned a road trip to visit the city of Colonia Tovar.

This city was known for its Black Forest atmosphere, with German architecture, shops, and wonderful restaurants. The area has rolling hills and indeed does reflect its European namesake area.

Four of us headed off the morning of the trip. I was driving, my wife was up front, and the Martinez clan, husband and wife, were in the back. We were making good time driving along the highway when traffic suddenly came to a halt. There was a military police roadblock.

Most cars were stopped, then quickly moved along after a brief conversation. A car with four Americans was interesting, so we were told to pull off to the side of the roadway. Two well-armed officers approached to speak with us. They asked who we were and where we were going.

I explained we were with the Tigres baseball team. Normally, that was more than enough to get us out of any pickle or questioning. The young officer was excited to hear we were part of the local professional baseball team. However, this was also an opportunity, he asked for our passports which we provided. Things were about to get complicated.

He addressed Mr. Martinez directly, but he did not speak Spanish. This visibly upset the officer, "How do you not speak Spanish?" he demanded. "Your name is Martinez. You are 'Latin' too!" he added forcibly. He obviously thought we were not being honest, so he called for assistance.

To set the changing scene, two armed officers were addressing us, and a third officer opposite had a rifle pointed at us. Not a comfortable situation, and my broken Spanish was not helping the situation. Thankfully, my wife was a fluent speaker of Spanish. After a few very tense moments, we were allowed to proceed, however, the officer still couldn't understand how a Latin-looking person named Martinez didn't speak Spanish.

We drove on and had a great day in Colonia Tovar. However, as we got onto the backroads to get there, we debated just going home. Nobody enjoyed having a rifle pointed at them. Thankfully, there were no more road stops.

Don't Forget to Say Grace

After working at quarry all those years, I earned some benefits. One of which was the ability to go out for lunch. Oh, there were plenty of business lunches, but most days I simply had lunch at my desk.

When I did want to go out for lunch, there were not a lot of options as we were located outside of town. There was a Burger King a couple of miles east which was rarely busy. I could drive down, go through the drive-through, and head back fairly quickly.

Normally, being hungry I would munch on a burger, fries, or nuggets on my way back to the office. After getting my lunch, I routinely pulled forward clearing the window, stopped and said a blessing for the food. This probably occurred once a week to break up my normal desk lunch routine.

On one particular day, I got my lunch, pulled forward, stopped, and closed my eyes. Suddenly, there were brakes squealing, crash noises, and loud banging. I opened my eyes, not believing what I was seeing. A car speeding through the restaurant parking lot lost control, hit two parked cars, went airborne, crossing the drive-through's exit lane, plowing through landscaping, going through a fence coming to a stop in the business' parking lot next door.

I cautiously drove forward, taking in all the damage. Was the driver okay? Looking to see, he was still trying to drive away. Part of the fence was attached to his badly damaged car but seeking a way out of the other parking lot.

Had I not paused to bless my food, my truck, driver's side, would have been in the direct path of the vehicle as it stormed its way across the drive-through exit. I stopped and changed my prayer to one of thanks for divine blessings.

Lesson learned: Remember to say grace. It may save your life.

Stop—Count Your Blessings

I was visiting Lake Tahoe in late May with my daughter. It snowed overnight, adding a beautiful touch to the Jeffrey and Ponderosa pines. Their dark green branches were now white with snow.

As a visitor from Florida, I thoroughly enjoyed the photo opportunities, however, I wanted no part of driving in snowy conditions. The roads were clear, no snow was forecast until late in the day, when we would be out of town.

We did some light hiking in the chill of the morning. It was fun to be the first ones to leave our tracks on the snow-covered trails. We had a busy day ahead, so after a few more pictures, we headed into town for an early lunch before pushing on.

Clouds began moving in while we were at lunch. I was getting nervous as our trip mapping had us going across a couple of mountain passes. My daughter and I were both checking our phones for weather and road updates. No alerts; all indications said we were good to go. As we started out, the roads were clear, and I finally started to relax.

We were doing well and had traveled about ten miles from town. We rounded a long curve on a mountainside when we entered a snow globe setting. There was light snow falling, snow was built up on the road, and I couldn't tell the edge of the road from the gulley beyond it. As the snowfall increased, we were searching for somewhere to turn around. There were vehicles behind us, so stopping to turn around was not an option.

We were on a two-lane road, my mind was spinning, and I knew to stay in the ruts made by other cars. Slowing my speed resulted in more traffic behind us. The clouds were darkening the sky. Still, there was no place to turn around, I'm driving, praying, and staying in my rut. What's that?

Oh no! What's that? I all but yelled. Ahead of us was a white car stopped in our lane. I started braking, but with the packed snow on the road, we continued heading directly toward the vehicle. Every muscle in my body was tensing up, we were slowing but there was no avoiding impact as we neared the stopped car, with no brake lights or flashers on. I noticed it was an Audi, its circles logo looked more like a target.

No traffic was approaching in the other lane, so I veered left to avoid a collision. Suddenly we were out of our rut, with our wheels no longer straight the snow took control of our steering. Our car was in a full sideways slide as we went around the stopped Audi. Frantically trying to regain control, I turned the steering wheel, suddenly we were sliding in the opposite direction, but crossing back into our lane. Thankfully, all the sliding in the snowpack slowed us significantly. We were still sideways and nearly stopped when we left the roadway. The snow was much deeper, we came to an abrupt stop, within a couple of feet of a steel pole.

I tried pulling out, but we were stuck. I looked at my stunned daughter; she asked if I was alright. Truth be known, *no*! Our car was stuck, off the roadway. We had no phone connectivity, snow was falling, then in the middle of my pity party, the white Audi just drove slowly past us. Were we okay? Did we need help? Nothing, just drove away… "No, I'm not okay. I am angry." My daughter's presence kept me from truly expressing my frustration.

After another minute to relax, I started to get out of the car and verify how bad everything was. A few people were coming to check on us. Then, for the first time, I looked down the road behind us: five vehicles were in the ditch, three pickups, two SUVs. One of the pickups was rolled over, and an SUV was on its side.

One man was telling me he was directly behind me, saw me spin out, then had to hit the ditch to avoid the Audi. His truck was flipped over, but his family was okay. The other vehicles, also unable to stop, opted for the ditch instead of colliding with the stopped car. Unbelievable! They were checking on me, and I'm feeling sorry for *myself.*

I hugged my daughter, looking down the road at all the vehicles, and said, "I need to relax, we were fortunate."

Other passing drivers slowed, asked about us, called the police, and confirmed the police were aware. An officer stopped, asking if there were any injuries, then said they were on another incident but would be back soon. I also learned when a snowplow is approaching to back away from his path, I was hit with a wave of snow, dirt, and debris. My Florida roots exposed.

It wasn't long before two officers arrived with four tow trucks close behind. After a quick assessment, an officer told me to get in the car, then he and several others gave us a push, and we came right up on the now plowed and clear roadway.

I bounced out to say thanks, he nodded but yelled, "Go, I've got all this traffic stopped."

We altered our driving plans, arriving at our destination late in the day, but there were no complaints. Looking back, wow, I don't want to do that again, but I learned to look at the entire picture before issuing the "Woe is me" cry, when I was actually "Wonderfully Blessed."

Heads Up and Just So You Know…

My son was sick, so I went to see him one afternoon at his mother's house in Miami. After a good visit, it was time to head home. I drove over to I-95, stopping at McDonald's on the way and headed north. Traffic was light even though it was early evening and not quite dark.

Approaching the Golden Glades interchange, I moved to the left lane to move onto the turnpike. The road was clear. I reached down to take a bit of my quarter pounder with cheese, when I slammed into something.

What had I hit? Nothing was in front of me and still wasn't. Slowing to a stop and moving off the road, my hood was buckled as I looked forward. On the dashboard was my burger, then I saw it, and fear went through my entire body.

On my car's antenna was a hand towel. Oh Lord, my only thought was I had hit someone and their vehicle as they were flagging traffic. No, it couldn't be! Please no! Scared to look, I walked to the front of my car. Was there blood? The impact was dead center of my front end.

Turning to look back down the highway, there was another crashed vehicle. What had I done? Where did it come from? I only looked down for a moment. Still, the question remained: where was the towel from, and did I hit a person flagging traffic?

As I walked back to the other vehicle, the police arrived, several cars were stopped, and there were clothes scattered all over the roadway. The first question was directed at me: Was I the other driver, and was I okay? "Yes, I'm good," I stammered. "Was anyone hurt?" not wanting to hear the answer. No, the driver is okay. Relief! Able to breathe, I just stood taking in the scene. Still asking myself, "What did I do?"

As I stood there lost in thought, a woman approached me, asking again if I was okay. I assured her I was okay. She then explained what occurred: she was behind me driving north. The other car came straight across the four lanes of the interstate from my right, adding, "I probably never saw the car till impact." She narrowly missed colliding with us and would have struck the other vehicle if I hadn't.

Wow, answers I needed, and she had already relayed this to the state police. The woman driving the other car was driving north from the Florida Keys and had everything she owned packed in her hatchback. My vehicle had completely knocked out the long sloping rear window, sending her clothes into flight and allowing a hand towel to wrap around my antenna.

In speaking with the woman, somehow getting home came up, and it turned out she also lived in Pembroke Pines. Not only that, but she also lived in the same community I did, only a couple of blocks away, and she offered to drive me home.

Once seated in her car, she gave me the following warning: "I work for the FBI and I'm packing, just so you know."

I never saw this lady again. Was she heaven sent? I don't know, but what are the odds that (1) she observed the entire accident scene, (2) she stopped to assist, (3) she spoke from a position of authority, (4) was a neighbor, dropping me at the door of my home. I won't know in this life, but I am grateful for the blessing.

Listen to That Inner Voice

Having grandchildren is one of the greatest joys of my life. They add so much to my life, both of my grandsons are active in youth sports, especially baseball. Just to play catch and run around with them makes any day better.

I was driving home from the ballfield one night after a game. The route takes me along an interstate and the speed limit reflects highway speed. I passed an exit, traffic merged and it's a good half mile to the first traffic light. I was traveling in the far left of four westbound lanes as I approached the red light.

Looking ahead several vehicles were in my lane, while only two were waiting in the lane to my right.

As I debated moving over to the less crowded lane, I heard a clear voice in my head "Stay in your lane." That was odd, but I wasn't in a hurry, so I stayed put, pulling up to the light and stopped. It wasn't ten seconds later, and *whoosh*!

A full-size pickup went by in that right lane at full speed, never stopping, crashing into the back vehicle, pushing it into the first car, knocking it into the intersection. Car parts were scattered across the roadway.

I was stunned. Had I not listened, I would have been vehicle taking the brunt of the impact. Surprisingly, no one appeared to be injured, but vehicles were totaled. The driver of the pickup appeared shaky but checking on him, he reeked of alcohol and his voice was slurred.

Where did the inner voice come from? I don't know, just glad I had listened and was grateful.

Just Enjoying My Lunch

In the summer of 2018, my daughter Macie and I traveled to the Canadian Rockies. What a beautiful part of the world, we were awed by nature from Banff to Jasper with several sidebar trips.

One of those day trips was to Lake Louise. We needed to park in a designated lot and take a shuttle bus to the lake. We were hurrying to catch the shuttle, then after walking across the parking lot to the bus stop; oops I left my camera in the car.

We returned to the car, I retrieved my camera from the trunk, then returned to the shuttle stop.

We rode the bus to the lake. It is a spectacular view. The large lake lined by mountains on the west, with Victoria Glacier clinging to their side. Opposite was a stately hotel and formal gardens along the lake. There are paths to walk the lakeside and even a trail up to a teahouse with views of the mountains, lake, and hotel.

After strolling the walkways, taking pictures, visiting the hotel, and just sitting taking in the views we headed back to the parking area. We had been out for over three hours. We walked across the parking lot talking about the beauty of all we had seen. Then looking toward the car, I exclaimed, "Oh No! The trunk is open."

We have all our luggage, jackets, souvenirs, and travel stuff in the trunk. Now it's standing wide open for the world to see, and we've been gone for hours. Hurrying to get there, amazingly everything seemed to be in place. We were double-checking, just saying "Wow," when someone called to us.

We turned to see a middle-aged man sitting in the car next to ours, windows down, eating a sandwich. "Hello," he said waving again. "I've just been sitting here watching your stuff and having lunch."

What did you say? "Yes, everything should be fine. I've had my eyes on your car." Wow, I was speechless. Then he started his car and began backing up. "Sir, thank you! Really, *thank you*!" I said.

He just waved, smiled while saying, "I've got places to be."

"What just happened?" I asked my daughter.

"That's crazy," she responded.

Make a note dear, "I think we were watched over by an angel."

OH, THOSE AWKWARD MOMENTS

We've all had those times when we wish we could disappear, saying not me, had to be someone else. I've had more than my share, these are just a few of my oops collection.

New Cellphone—Poor Excuse

Receiving a new cell phone can be an adventure; transferring data, pictures, and it seems something is always lost, or we end up calling wrong numbers. This was never more evident than when my flip phone was upgraded to a newer model.

My phone was provided through my employer, which was a nice benefit. No cost and the occasional upgrade, but I was expected to be available for customers and work-related calls. The downside of being a manager of a department working 24-7 was phone calls day and night. The only time I didn't have my phone was when attending church; it stayed in the truck, no exception.

A longtime sales manager and friend of many years had suddenly and totally unexpectedly passed away from a heart attack. He had symptoms throughout the day and, like too many of us, ignored them until it was too late. He was well-known, so when his viewing was scheduled, there were a large number of people attending to share condolences and stories.

We were having a busy night in the railyard; there had been a breakdown, now the railroad was dragging their feet providing railcars to load. My night shift supervisor was new in his position, didn't handle stress very well, and had called me several times since I had left the yard.

With this in mind, I made sure my new cell phone was on vibrate mode as I slipped it into my pants pocket as I walked in from the overflowing parking lot. The funeral home was of good size, but with all the family and friends, it was near capacity. I spoke with many people, all saddened at our friend's passing.

After a few minutes, I made it to the front of the room, speaking with his wife and family. The open casket was rightly surrounded by many floral arrangements. I took my place in a steady line of people approaching the casket. Just as I started forward, I felt my cell phone vibrating and could hear a low buzz. Without looking, I deftly slipped my hand into my pocket to disconnect the call. Ahh, silence. I was alone beside the casket.

"Hello, hello!" my phone was saying. I looked around, as did others.

Then, even louder and frustratedly, "HELLO! ARE YOU THERE!" Suddenly, I recognized the voice; it was my supervisor, and he was upset.

Now yelling through my phone, as I desperately grabbed at my phone, "HELLOOO! HELLOOO! CAN'T YOU HEAR ME? HELLO!" everyone was staring at me. Who is the guy at the casket? What is he thinking?

Finally, I got the call disconnected, put the phone back in my pocket, turned away from the casket, and tried to act like nothing was going on. My phone vibrated again.

I didn't touch my pocket or reach for my phone. I apologized to a family member and left soon afterward. To this day, I've never taken my cell phone into a funeral home again.

Courtesy Is the Best Policy

In the late eighties, I worked full-time, putting in some long hours. Additionally, I was attending college, working toward completing my bachelor's degree. Most of my classes were taken in the evening, two or three days a week. I really looked forward to the weekend so I could catch up and get some rest.

I was also active in my church, working with adult singles and single parents. Our pastor was very caring, wanting to encourage and assist single parents. He started a program to bring in local community leaders monthly to do so.

One of the first speakers was going to be Dr. Bob Barnes. He is highly regarded in the Christian community, an author of several books on parenting, marriage, and family, and started a ministry for troubled youth and their families. We had promoted the event for several weeks and were looking forward to a wonderful evening of discussion and fellowship. I was asked to introduce the guest speaker.

The meeting was scheduled in the evening. I had a late afternoon class at the main college campus in Boca Raton. It was going to be a close call at best to be on time. It is just over thirty miles from the campus to the church. Class should end just after six, hurry to my car, head to Interstate 95, pray for minimal traffic, then Pembroke Road all the way to the church. The program was to start at seven; it was doable, but there were a lot of factors at play.

The day arrived, class was dismissed at 6:05 p.m. There was a five-minute hustle to my car; I was finally onto the interstate, and things were looking okay. Traffic was not heavy; things were breaking my way. I turned onto Pembroke Road with fifteen minutes for the normally ten-minute drive. I caught a few traffic lights and was getting anxious. Pembroke is a four-lane divided main street. I needed to relax and just drive.

As I got closer to the church, I noticed a green station wagon in the lane beside me. The driver and I made eye contact. It was obvious he wanted to move into the left lane, which is where I was. The driver all but asked me if I would let him in. No way! I was on a mission, had a job to do, and needed to make a left myself.

He gave one more plea, but I said, "Not a chance, buddy." As I waited for traffic to clear to make a left into the church, I noticed the station wagon turn in on the other side of the church.

My efforts had paid off. It was three minutes to seven, and I was safely parked outside the church. Things were rolling my way.

As I headed inside, saying hello, letting others know I'm present, I asked if Dr. Barnes was there so I could meet him before the introduction. I was surprised to hear he wasn't there yet. Then someone said, "Oh, there's Dr. Barnes," looking across the room, there was the driver of the station wagon, Dr. Bob Barnes.

It was just moments later; I was called on to introduce our guest speaker. As I got to the front of the room, I told the gathering I had met Dr. Barnes just minutes earlier, explaining my actions and apologizing. He was very generous, laughing it off, and I was humbled. I still struggle occasionally with road grumpiness.

After making amends, the next monthly meeting was going well. I had learned the guest speaker was the father of a new baby. I surprised him with a gift from our group. He opened the cute dress outfit to oohs and awws. He turned to me, smiling, and graciously said, "Ron, I don't know how my son will look in this?"

Always Expect the Unexpected

As a member of The Gideons International, I have the opportunity to speak in local evangelical Christian churches. It is a privilege to do so, and worshipping with others strengthens one's walk with the Lord.

All churches are unique, from pulpit to sound systems. The length of the talk varies depending on the church. I've spoken for three minutes to thirty minutes; however, we must respect the time allotted and not go overtime.

I like to look at the speaking podium before the service. Such was the case recently; the pulpit was elevated which changed the look as I addressed the congregation. Otherwise, everything seemed normal. I was introduced according to the program and was to talk for twelve minutes.

Things were going as planned. I like to step away from the podium as I talk, which allows me to better engage the congregation. As I stepped away, I heard the air conditioner turn on, and the cool air blew down and felt great. However, as I glanced back toward the pulpit, my notes were blowing off the pulpit and with the added height, they were floating like leaves in the wind.

Well, the laughter was different, and an usher handed me a few pages that were off the platform. The talk finished as scheduled, but the people may have remembered the flying papers more than my presentation. Always be prepared.

I Made the Sports Page

Looking back at my time as an athletic trainer, it was a wonderful job, and I occasionally wonder how my life would be had I remained with sports at the professional or college level. However, it also made for a forgettable moment.

Our team was playing the Yankees in Fort Lauderdale. The complex was the spring training home for the major league team for many decades. The ballpark was compact and drew good crowds during the Florida State League season.

It was a warm South Florida summer night; the game was in the later innings. Those of us not playing would watch from the dugout and frequently munch on sunflower seeds. It was this night when suddenly one of our batters got hit in the rib cage with a pitched ball and went down on one knee.

I had just thrown a handful of sunflower seeds into my mouth. Up the steps of the dugout, hustling toward home plate, while trying to move the seeds to one side of my mouth so I could talk with the batter.

Then, just before I reached the injured player, I tripped, falling face first, sliding into the batter's box. Now covered in clay, I tried to quickly get to my feet, but I had swallowed nearly all the sunflower seeds along with their shells. I was choking, couldn't breathe, or get a word out. Thankfully, the batter was okay; he, the catcher, umpire, and fans were all having a good laugh.

The batter finally gave me a couple of blows on my back, which helped as I was spitting seeds and bent over. Afterward, I brushed myself off, waved to the crowd, and headed back to a still laughing, reenacting dugout. I just wanted some water.

The next day, the Fort Lauderdale *Sun Sentinel* newspaper concluded their story on the game with a description of the Orioles Trainer's dramatic slide at home plate.

Lesson learned: Only a couple of sunflower seeds at a time.

Should We Always Follow Our Parents' Example?

How many times have I heard "Parents are role models"? As a child, it was, "Watch, listen, and learn from your mom and dad. What would your dad do?" Then as a parent, "Set a good example. Your children are always watching you." Even now as a grandparent, I am aware of my grandsons observing me to see how to act.

Growing up, our family was always engaged with many other families, whether it was church activities, neighbors gathering, Dad's coworkers, or relatives. As a child, I learned certain hierarchies, one of which was when traveling by car, men sat in the front, women in the back seat, and kids were in the third seat of the station wagon.

In the spring of tenth grade of high school, I had my first dates. I drove my dad's old pickup truck. I picked up my date, said hello to her parents, and drove to a bowling alley where we met others to enjoy being out together.

Then I was selected to be a prom server for the high school prom. This was a real honor because very few sophomores attended the prom. It also happened that the young lady I had dated twice was also selected. We were going to attend together, and being it was the prom, one of my friends said we could make it a double date; he would drive his nice car.

My friend came by the house; we headed off to pick up my date. I was excited to be attending the prom—it was the spring highlight at school, and I was going. We got to my date's home, and everyone was giddy. After all, it was the prom. After saying our goodbyes to her parents, we headed to the car.

I held the door as she slid into the back seat and closed the door for her. I walked around the car, smiling at her still-watching parents, and happily got into the front seat next to my friend, oblivious to his shocked face. I remember waving to her parents just as we backed away; they looked sort of startled. I turned to continue our conversation, but nobody was talking except me.

We drove on to pick up my friend's prom date. As we all got out to greet her, he grabbed me and said forcibly, "You're sitting in the *back* seat with your date!"

Suddenly, it hit me, why all the looks, the hurt in her eyes, but I only did what guys do, right?

The Rest of the Story

It was a long night at the prom. I didn't know how to make up for my mistake. We did the required server task together, but then it was over. My date spent the rest of the evening with her sister, who was a senior, taking away from her prom night also. Then to finalize the night, my partner informed me she would be riding home with her sister and her sister's boyfriend. I got the "You're sitting in the backseat by yourself" treatment on the way home.

Yes, I was clueless, totally naive to the point of not even knowing to be embarrassed. However, we did date again, even attending the prom as juniors.

I never told my dad this story, maybe the only time I ever followed his lead and messed up.

HEY, REF!

I've noted in other stories how my dad was active in sports, but he was also an umpire and basketball referee. For many years, he officiated basketball, and he was exceptional at blowing the whistle.

He did it for two reasons: one, it was good exercise and he enjoyed it. Secondly, it helped in providing for our family. I remember when living in Virginia Beach, Dad would call an evening basketball game and occasionally stop at the Pine Tree Inn on the way home, buying a pizza for him and Mom to share. As a child, I was supposedly asleep, but the smell of the pizza would fill the house.

I also got to attend a few of his games in Virginia and then more later in Florida. He sent me up in the stands and always told me not to say I was the official's son.

It was always enjoyable to go. I never turned down an opportunity.

Years later, while having dinner with friends, I was introduced to their neighbor. He happened to be a referee and the president of the local High School Basketball Officials Organization. He said they were always looking for referees and gave me their contact information.

After much thought and for the same reasons as my dad, I registered with the state and the local basketball officials' association. Attended a series of clinics to study the rules and how to apply them during a game. I ordered a uniform, shoes, and a whistle. I informed my dad; he encouraged me to give it a shot. Let's play ball.

My first game was a junior varsity game at Westwood Christian School. I called the game with Ralph, a much more experienced official. At the end of the first quarter, we talked for a moment. He let me know it was okay to blow my whistle if the ball went out of bounds, a violation occurred, or there was a foul. Over the years, I called many games with Ralph, but looking back, he totally carried me throughout that first game.

I officiated over twenty games during that first year, but I was still totally green. I had a lot of learning ahead. That first year, I only called small private school junior varsity games, which is where my game belonged.

Toward the end of my second year, a special opportunity occurred. My mom and dad came down from Central Florida for a visit. Dad and I talked occasionally about how I was coming along as an official. I was scheduled for a junior varsity game at Columbus High School. Now I had a chance to run the floor and he could sit in the stands watching me.

The game tipped off. I was surprised how nervous I was. The game was very physical, we misapplied some basic rules, both coaches were yelling at us. In the second half, even though I was working with a more experienced official, our performance got worse. I charged a coach with a technical foul for questioning calls; moments later, my partner threw him out of the game. It was ugly.

After the game, Dad and I had a long forty-minute ride back to the house. I remember thinking beforehand about ordering pizza on the way home. That wasn't going to happen. Finally, I asked Dad what he thought about the game and hinted about the officiating. He loved me too much to say what he really thought. However, he made it clear, beating around the bush, asking questions, encouraged me to stick with it, and advised me to watch veteran officials. I know he didn't tell anyone in the stands he was the referee's dad. It was the only game he ever got to watch me officiate. But I reassured him from time to time I was improving. He would just smile, giving me the "I sure hope so" look.

Over the years, officiating was good for my physical health, kept me in shape, and provided a few funds for the family, especially at Christmas. One December, I worked a doubleheader and purchased a Christmas bicycle for my son. A few years later, I took a vacation day from work, called three games that day, and bought Christmas bikes for my daughters.

I was blessed that day; in the final game, one team was a big underdog, so to keep the game close, they decided to hold the ball. The score at halftime was like 4 to 6; both teams were content to let the clock run, and so was I. Thank You, Lord.

I did develop into a much better referee over the years. Moved up to calling all varsity games and began officiating deeper into the post-season playoffs. Then, after nearly twenty-five years, the assignments came out for the Florida State High School Basketball Tournament Finals. I was heading to Lakeland to call a state semi-final game, Winter Haven versus Leesburg, both schools being from the area would ensure a good crowd.

Wow, I was invited to the state tournament. Lakeland is only thirty-five miles from home. I learned of the assignment on Monday and the game was Thursday night. I so much wanted to call my dad, personally invite him, but he had passed away and would be watching from heaven. I still had a lot of family living in the area, but I made the decision to stay quiet and drive home Friday morning. I needed to stay focused on the task at hand.

As I drove to Lakeland, my mind rewound, so many games over the years, the officials who mentored me. I was excited, but I knew I had to just stay calm and call the game. I checked into the hotel, it was beside the arena, caught up with my officiating partners. Both had previously called several state games; we knew each other and had refereed many times together.

We walked over to the arena early, as state veterans, they knew there would be a buffet available to us to eat. We checked in, were given gifts to recognize our state finals participation. Everything was first-class. I munched on a few things, wasn't about to eat. My partners just chowed down. A state official came in and reviewed the pregame schedule.

We walked out onto the floor, took our positions on the court. As the clock wound down, we talked with the captains, the teams left the floor, and we were called off also. The state official apologized for being late, but we needed to put on some electronics which would start and stop the clock on our whistle. It went on our waistline, and a wire ran under our shirts up to be clipped on near our neck opening. Getting tucked back in, it was time to return from this alcove to the floor.

We took our place on the court together for the National Anthem. I thought about my dad, gave a squeeze to one of his old whistles I was carrying in my pocket. The teams were introduced, followed by our names as officials being announced. I had made it. Now, it was game time. We shook hands, let's go.

The game got off to a good start, both teams playing under control. It is easier to officiate a game with good teams and players knowing what they were doing. There was an enthusiastic crowd cheering, the game was moving along.

Midway through the second quarter, I blew my whistle, calling a foul and headed to the area to report the foul. A person at the table was waving to me and wanted to speak to me. I'm thinking we've overlooked something; I step closer and say, "What's up?"

He replies, "You know this game is on TV? Right?"

I answer "Yes, I'm aware of that." Actually, it was my first live TV game, I thought it was pretty cool.

He turned serious, almost to a glare, saying, "Will you please zip up your pants? You are a distraction!"

Looking down, I saw he was right—while putting that last minute equipment on, I left my zipper wide open.

Back to the game, I looked at my partners, and they had big smiles on their faces. "Rookie!" We had a good laugh at halftime.

The game was close and finished with no further incidents involving the officiating crew.

What a great experience, but it's good to be brought back to reality, sometimes.

The Rest of the Story

The morning after the tournament, I drove home to Webster, seeing Mom, sharing with her where I'd been and that I carried Dad's whistle. She gave me a mom hug—that was all I needed. I was very blessed!

Later that weekend, I shared my story with other family members and friends.

Even when returning for the next basketball season and being recognized for officiating at the state tournament by the local association, the zipper story was told by others.

When you referee a basketball or umpire a baseball game, know the color of your pants. I had black underwear on, but the white stripes of my shirt were glowing. Live and learn! Keep your zipper zipped!

I never got back to the state finals in Lakeland but called plenty of other playoff games. My career ended after thirty-four years because of my knees, which wore out with all the running up and down the hardwood. Additionally, to be honest, as I got older, I didn't have the same patience with coaches or players. It was time to stop, it was great fun while it lasted and met needs.

OH, WHAT A NIGHT

As a basketball referee, I saw many situations and occurrences during ballgames. However, just when you think you've seen it all, the totally unexpected may happen. Thus, it was this night.

I was assigned to officiate a game late in the season between two rival high schools. Over the years, I had called several games at both of their home sites. This evening's game would draw a bigger crowd because of the rivalry, but nobody was expecting a close game.

The home team was loaded with talent, had the county's leading scorer, a winning record, and was looking forward to the upcoming state playoffs. Meanwhile, the visitors were not very good, with only a couple of wins, and were just playing the season out.

The home team's site was not far from home and close to several places to eat afterward. I asked my fiancée to attend the game with me and go to dinner postgame. She had played sports in high school and was familiar with both schools.

Arriving at the school, I was surprised to find the parking lot nearly full and a larger than expected attendance. This was a great sign; I was explaining to my fiancé how I thought a large crowd added to the atmosphere, making the game more enjoyable. She was seated in the upper rows of the bleachers; I could see her clearly while I was on the court.

The game got off to the expected start, the home team was quickly ahead. From a referee's perspective, it was a clean game. The visitors were unable to put up much of a fight and the star of the home team was having another good night scoring. At halftime, the home team was ahead by more than twenty points.

The second half started much like a continuation of the first. The home team was in control... But *then* it happened. The star player for the home team made a long three-point shot... Rolls of toilet paper came flying out of the stands onto the court. Unrolling as they were thrown high into the air, creating long tails, it was quite a sight. The bored crowd enjoyed the moment, laughing, and a few even applauding.

We assessed the home team a technical foul for the actions of the crowd and the delay of game. Nobody seemed bothered as the eight or more rolls were cleared from the court. As mentioned above, it had provided a highlight in an otherwise ordinary game.

The emotion of the game was unchanged, but that was about to change. Following the flow of the players down the floor, still early in the third quarter, the visiting team coach jumped up requesting a timeout. The rules that season didn't allow coaches to call timeouts. However, he was emphatic. I had known him for several years and sensed something was wrong. I blew my whistle to stop the clock and grant the timeout.

Immediately, his players from the bench bolted across the floor into the stands. Turning, I saw the home team's players were charging the stands also. Suddenly, there was a huge fight in the stands. My fiancé was sitting just above the fray, but I could no longer see her.

I started to head that way when my partner grabbed my arm.

I yelled in protest, "I've got to ..."

He tightened his grip, saying, "There ain't nobody over there who likes you!"

We stood on the court as the police arrived, breaking up the fighting. Fans from each school were directed to different sides of the court. The visiting fans were sent home and had to clear the parking lot. They were then followed by the home fans, the police ensuring everyone was gone.

During this delay, the administrator of the home team's school came out to speak to my partner and me. He asked if we were okay. After assuring him we were fine, he chastised us for not controlling the fans in the stands. I just rolled my eyes, holding my tongue, as officials we are responsible for the action on the court, not in the bleachers.

After the game, I learned from my fiancé that a couple of students were goofing around, throwing a roll of toilet paper back and forth. When one ducked, the roll hit the girlfriend of a fan from the other school, starting the fracas.

Once the all-clear was given, the game resumed; with only the two teams, cheerleaders, the administrator, and my girlfriend, the only person in the stands.

The balance of the game was uneventful. The home team continued to score points at will, winning easily by over thirty points.

As we were exiting the gym, there was still a heavy police presence in the parking area. They were concerned about getting all the home team players safely off-site and the visitor's bus securely on its way.

The worst part of a game with a fight, ejection, or unexpected delay is all the paperwork and reports. This one was extraordinary with multiple letters for the local associations and state.

The Rest of the Story

In my thirty-four years of officiating, this night stands apart. I saw complete darkness during a power outage, upset coaches and players, heard chants of fans, and saw amazing play. However, when a very ordinary game is interrupted by the toilet paper toss and unfortunate gym clearing fight, it stands alone. It was also the only game my soon to be wife ever attended while I officiated.

Additionally, more than twenty-five years later, I was talking to a new member at church when it was discovered he was the school administrator from that night. His recollection of the night's events are a little different than mine, but we agreed it was a night we won't ever forget.

AN INTRODUCTION
TO SKIING

I first traveled to Innsbruck, Austria, in 1978. We were driving around Europe, and having seen the 1976 Winter Olympics, it was a place I wanted to visit. The city, surrounded by snow-topped mountains, was warm and welcoming. It was mid-September; the air was cool and crisp.

I remember visiting an Olympic site, seeing the ski jumping hills used during the games. Being in awe, I got into a crouch position, imagining myself gliding down the ramp, hitting the take-off table, flying through the air to a perfect landing. Everyone laughed, as I'd never snow skied in my life, but one day I wanted my Franz Klammer moment. (He is an Austrian Winter Olympics hero).

Nearly ten years later, a group of friends from church were talking about going skiing. We lived in South Florida, and had water skied together several times, on one occasion earning a lifelong nickname.

"Oh no," I was told, "We are planning a trip to Innsbruck to snow ski."

"What?" I was at once interested and excited. "Yes, we are working with a travel agent, who's putting together a good package."

"You've got to come with us. Danny has never skied either. We'll take turns teaching you guys. It's easy!"

The trip was booked, with six of us flying to Munich in early March, taking a tour bus to Innsbruck. Once in Innsbruck, we'd rent a minivan and be on our own. There were six members of our team, "the Pups," a married couple and experienced skiers. "Wild Bill," another good skier, would be my roommate. Danny's son had limited ability but was a quick learner. Danny, in his early forties, and I, in my thirties, had never strapped on the wooden planks and had very little snow experience.

The months went by quickly, and we arrived in Austria to fresh snowfall. The next morning, we headed to the ski rental shop to get outfitted with our skis for the week. Having our equipment in hand, it was time to go have some fun.

Day 1

Driving from the city to the ski resort, everyone was laughing and making jokes. After parking, with our lift passes in hand, we started for the first ski lift. We put our skis on and began our awkward walk and slide to ride the lift. I fell at least twice moving along the line, quickly stepped into position, and the chair swept us up and into the air.

Once at the top, it was beautiful, with a brilliant sun shining against the backdrop of snow-covered trees and blue skies. Danny and I were told to listen up; it was class time. We were standing at the start of an intermediate run, and there was only one way down—on our skis.

It is important to clarify a couple of things now that we are on the mountain top. Intermediate ski runs in Europe could easily be classified as blue or black or expert runs in the United States. Kids in Alpine areas are skiing by age two, without poles, and quickly develop into competent skiers.

One of the "Pups" and Wild Bill took turns giving Danny and me instructions—getting into a wedge, skiing across the slope to control speed, how to stand back up after falling. "Relax! Don't fight it! Don't turn uphill!" Then it would start all over again. "Get into a wedge! Don't point the skis downhill! Relax, Ron, relax!"

As we struggled, others were zipping by us, laughing and enjoying the day. Our team kept rotating off as instructors; whoever wasn't teaching was flying down the run, returning to say how wonderful the conditions were. Well, Danny and I were covered in snow from fall after fall, retrieving skis; and it gets very cold when more time is spent on your butt than upright on your skis.

In all honesty, I don't know how long that first ski run was, but it was a good two hours before we made it to the base of the run. Exhausted from constant falls and climbing back onto our skis, our teaching team told us we did great. "Are you ready to go again?" I truly think if Danny or I had the car keys, we would have been hotel-bound… No, we needed to rest and warm up.

Carrying our skis, we walked a hundred yards or so toward the resort hub. "What the heck!" We both yelled simultaneously. "What is that?"

On our left was a large wide bunny hill a few hundred yards long. The gentle slope was virtually empty. Really! We couldn't believe what we were seeing. No, we didn't go running for more practice; Danny and I sat down at the café. Rested, relaxed, and rested some more. Skiing can wear you out.

That afternoon, I lived on the gentle terrain of the beginner hill. I must confess the lessons learned that morning made gliding down with very few crashes enjoyable. Maybe, I can do this ski thing.

Day 3

After two days of practice and encouragement, I was finally able to ride the lift to the top of the run and make it to the bottom with minimal falls. Oh, I was far from perfect, but skiing was finally enjoyable. I was able to glide slowly downhill, look up, and take in the beauty of the mountain scenery.

Danny and I still partnered together, primarily in case one of us took the big tumble. We had learned to read trail maps and stayed on the easy runs. The rest of our team was all over the different resorts we were visiting.

On a midmorning run, we were both gliding down the mountain when a large group of preschool kids came zipping down the run. They were no more than four or five years of age; they skied around and between us, laughing and enjoying a day on the slopes. I couldn't help but believe they were having fun at our expense.

Looking down the hill, I noticed the class had stopped to rest on the left side of the run. Danny and I caught up with them while maintaining our modified wedge ski style. Just as we got in front of the group, we skied toward one another as we crisscrossed the hill. Neither one of us could move out of the other's way. Oh no, we skied into each other, going too slow to crash and fall, we slid together standing chest to chest.

Our audience couldn't believe it; they were roaring with laughter, pointing, and enjoying the show. To make matters worse, we couldn't separate ourselves, standing on each other's skis, we looked as if we were stuck together. The kids loved it, but I couldn't understand a word they were shouting.

Finally, after what seemed like an eternity pushing against each other without success, we opted to just fall over in order to separate. This thrilled the students; some actually applauded as they stood, took one more smiling look at us, and headed down the run. Truth be known, Danny and I were laughing too.

Our Final Ski Day

We were having a great week in Innsbruck, spending all day on the mountains, and relaxing together at night planning the next day. The people of the area being so open and friendly added joy to our adventure.

We were active members of our church in South Florida. In the months leading up to our trip, I reached out to a Christian missionary in the Innsbruck area. I had explained a group of us were coming on a ski trip and would like to meet with him one day.

It was decided we would have dinner together one evening after our day of skiing. Our team was looking forward to getting together and had asked him if there was anything we could bring him from home. He gave us a simple request but added he had made it before with no success.

On our last day, we had decided to ski at Axamer Lizum, a large resort with a lot of runs for all ability levels. It was a busy day and thousands of skiers had decided to hit the slopes. The runs were spread across the mountain, so while skiing, you never realized it was busy. There was plenty of room for me to glide, take in the scenery, fall, and go again.

It was early afternoon, I found myself on a wonderful run, it was wide, with a moderate grade, and as far as I could see, there were no turns. There were only a handful of skiers that I could see. It was wide-open ski perfection.

As I started down the slope, my mind flashed back to Franz Klammer. Suddenly, I was transported to the Olympics; it was my final run of the downhill competition, and I had to win. I pointed my skis straight down the mountain, got into a tuck position, saying to myself, "How fast can I go!" I zipped past several other skiers; I was flying down the mountain, tears were forming in my eyes. Wow! This is awesome!

Then just as quickly, I came to my senses, "What am I doing!" racing downhill? I had gone hundreds of yards in the tuck position. I don't know how to stop, not at this speed. I tried to stand upright, but that wasn't working. I could see the end of the run in the distance. I needed to slow down; I was at rocket speed.

No answers were coming into my head; beginning to panic, I tried standing again. No way! Then, seeing more skiers ahead, I was in the tight tuck position, so I just fell over. My skis broke free, I tumbled and rolled, *but* I stopped.

That was uncontrolled chaos. I had my moment but didn't want any part of it again. I retrieved my skis, got them back on, and glided to the bottom of the run as if nothing had happened. Several people were gawking at me as I returned to the lift line, headed out of the area, thankful I was in one piece.

We finished our day of skiing; everyone was feeling good about the week we'd had. A few wanted to extend our stay, but we had a dinner to attend.

We had agreed to meet at a restaurant the missionary and his wife had chosen. It was a spectacular setting on a hilltop overlooking a snow-covered valley, and the meal was equally as good. We had a great time, talking and learning about their work. They invited us back to their home for dessert and coffee.

They were from Texas, and the one request he had was for chips and salsa. They indicated that in the eighties, they couldn't be found in Austria. I recalled when we were departing for the airport, saying to the Pups, "What's the heavy-duty cardboard box for?" They indicated it was the chips. I had brought the salsa, wrapping the glass jars in my thick ski socks.

While we ate delicious cheesecake and our new friend sat eating chips and salsa. Content as we all were, he thanked us, saying whenever he'd been given chips in the past, they were like sawdust because of the travel.

They introduced us to their twelve-year-old son, saying he was an exceptional skier. Then he asked him where he skied today. He replied, "Axamer Lizum." To which he asked if he had seen any of us on the mountain today.

The youngster took a long look at the six of us, then pointed at me and began to laugh. He said, "I saw him!" He started to leave the room as everyone joined in the laughter.

"Wait!" I called out. "There were thousands of people on the mountain today. You're saying you saw me?"

Yes, and he went on to describe what I was wearing. Nailed! Laughing harder, he exited the room. Thankfully, he didn't address my ski ability.

The Rest of the Story

The missionary we visited with was named Charlie Brown. He and his wife were wonderful people. All of us regretted not getting together earlier in the week and more than once.

What a fantastic week in Innsbruck. We had a great time enjoying the beauty of the mountains and fellowshipping.

By the way, a year later I took my eight-year-old son skiing. Yes, he went to Ski School.

THE FAMILY HITS
THE SLOPES

Living in beautiful but flat South Florida, when it comes to vacation time, we frequently looked to the mountains. In the winter that means snow skiing. Another chapter documents my first ski adventure, but as my children grew, it was time for them to strap on their skies and head downhill.

The year after my experience in Innsbruck, my son and I headed to Winter Park, Colorado. Chatter had informed me they had a very good ski school, he learned quickly. We had a great time and by week's end we were skiing together.

My skiing ability was also increasing, proof of this once again came from a class of children. As glided downhill there was light snow falling, filling my beard, I paused to relax momentarily, when a class from the ski school zipped past. Once I started back down the slope, I caught up with the class which had stopped for a rest, the teacher called to them, saying "Watch out! Here comes Santa Claus!" This was a big improvement from my last interaction with a ski class, but I still drew laughter.

The following stories are just a few highlights of family ski adventures.

Who Is Your Teacher?

As my daughters grew up, their turn on the slopes came about. Once again, as they were first-timers, we headed to Winter Park. We had a nice room with a kitchen, living area, and a large loft. Because we arrived later in the day and had no time for grocery shopping, I got up early and headed out to the shuttle bus stop to go into town to get breakfast. It was cold as I waited, waited, and waited. Finally, a car stopped, the driver asked if I was waiting for the shuttle. "Yes," I replied, shivering… "It's Sunday, buddy, the bus won't be by for another hour." Not a great start to the week, Dad.

After breakfast, we headed to the slopes, and my daughters were entered into ski school. They were enjoying daily classes; we could stop by, watch them on the enclosed bunny hills. Eventually, they moved out to easy runs—their favorite was called "Ski Papa."

Early in the week, after returning from the slopes, they were talking excitedly about their ski day. However, they kept talking about "Mr. Potato Head." Finally, I had to ask, "Who is Mr. Potato Head?"

"He is our teacher," came the innocent reply.

"Excuse me," I said empathically, "You don't call your teacher Mr. Potato Head." They protested, saying that was the instructor's name. "No, nobody is named Mr. Potato Head," I was trying hard not to be frustrated. "I don't want to hear it again, understood? It's disrespectful."

Unknown to the family, when I was in the eighth grade, the neighbor living across the street was called "Mr. Potato Head." My group of friends said he had been a teacher, was far from beloved, and was on the wrong end of many jokes and pranks. I was new in town and had no knowledge of him, but I knew if I called an adult "Mr. Potato Head," I would have been in the doghouse.

The girls picked up the art of skiing, like their brother before them. Quickly, they were riding lifts and barreling downhill by the end of the week.

Late in the week, I was picking up the girls and had an opportunity to talk with an instructor about their progress. He came across the room introducing himself: "Hi, I'm Mr. Potato Head," he said, smiling. "It's easy for the kids to remember, and we fist bump or do a mashed potato depending on how they're doing."

I didn't say anything to him, but I think he knew about my ultimatum. He spoke highly of the girls and their progress. I thanked him, telling him the entire school staff was appreciated.

That evening at dinner as the family ate, I ate crow and apologized. We still laugh when sharing memories of that family ski trip, and Mr. Potato Head always comes up.

A Bucket List Ride

Growing up in the sixties, Saturday afternoon meant the *Wide World of Sports* would be on TV. They covered all kinds of major and off-beat sports, from bull riding to barrel jumping; they covered it all. The classic byline of the show was "the thrill of victory and the agony of defeat." Curt Gowdy was the host, and if it was on the air, I was glued to the TV with anticipation.

Living in warm-weather states, I was drawn to the outdoor winter sports. Snow skiing and ski jumping were near the top of my favorites list. However, the sport I desired to watch more than any other was the bobsled, two- or four-man, it didn't matter. Seeing the specialized sleds race down frozen tracks, gliding through tight curves, the crew pushing at the start, then leaning in unison one way and then the other, always with their heads down, saving hundredths of a second on their time. Wow, it was fantastic.

Many amusement parks and county fairs had bobsled rides. Climbing into the sled-shaped car, I would be thinking of the real deal, sliding along, trying not to hit the sidewalls, gaining speed. The circular fair ride would force me against the side of the sled, give some ups and downs, but never satisfy my thirst for the "Real McCoy." Maybe one day, I'll keep dreaming. *Whoosh!*

Oh, with every thrill of victory, there was the agony of defeat. A team would come up just short of winning, going high into turns or a poor push to start the run. Of course, there were the dramatic failures, a sled exiting the track or, more commonly, a sled flipping over on its side, a very dangerous situation. The most famous of these happened to the Jamaican bobsled team during the 1988 Olympics in Calgary, Canada. The team flipped onto its side coming out of a curve and continued down the track through other turns before stopping. Amazingly and thankfully, no one was injured.

When preparing for my first ski trip to Innsbruck just a month later, we heard the public could take a ride on the Olympic track there. Our group was all in on giving it a try. Unfortunately, the track closed for the season the week before we arrived. This was my chance; I just missed out, but I'll keep dreaming.

While planning a family ski vacation in 2005, the decision was made to go to Park City, Utah. It had easy access from Salt Lake City, three ski areas offered nearby slopes, and I had skied there previously with my son. After setting up the trip, I was watching sports; they were bobsledding at the Utah Olympic Park in Park City. This was my opportunity, and I wasn't about to let it slip through my fingers a second time. *Game on!*

All the necessary information was on their website. I made reservations to ride the bobsled on our midweek down day. Thus began the countdown; it went from months to weeks, to days, to hours.

The course is approximately a mile long, with fifteen sweeping turns, downhill all the way. Riding the bobsled, operated by an experienced driver, flying down the icy track, where it would take hundreds of yards to stop at top speeds. My turn was coming.

The family rode the shuttle to Utah Olympic Park; I was fired up, leaning one way then hard back the other way, as if I was in the sled, but irritating the kids.

My daughters were too young to ride, but they could go through the orientation process with us. My daughters' mother, my son, the driver, and I would make up the four-person sled crew. We all attended the information session, which detailed the many hazards of bobsledding. Several people withdrew after watching the flipping bobsleds and out-of-control incidents on the video. Afterward, we signed the releases stating we knew the sport was dangerous.

While selecting our helmets, we were introduced to our driver. He encouraged us, explaining he had years of experience, and then he added he was the Olympic coach of the Jamaican Bobsled Team. Really, the team that flipped their sled, slid sideways through turns, before coming to a stop. Yes, he acknowledged, but he wasn't the driver. The first sense of apprehension entered my mind.

We hugged our daughters, posed for a picture, helmets on, and climbed into the sled. Easier said than done, it was a tight fit, we were told to keep our heads down and hold tight to the small handles. It was go time!

A couple of assistants gave us the push start; we were moving down the track, no stopping us now. It was a bumpy beginning; there is no comfort in the sled. We began to pick up speed, trying to look ahead to anticipate turns was impossible.

Just keep your head down. Into the first turn, now we were moving, I could feel my body being pushed into the bottom of the sled—*whoosh*—we were whipped back the other way.

We were zooming down the track, sliding through curves, my mind racing as fast as the sled. Although it was a clear sunny day, it was like midnight on the course, I couldn't see to anticipate anything. *Whoosh!* Another curve bouncing us side to side. Our speed continued to increase, the G-forces making my lower back ache. *Whoosh!* Turns were coming quick and hard. *Whoosh!* My lower back was killing me. *Whoosh!* We whipped the other direction.

O Lord, I was beginning to pray. *Whoosh!* Faster yet, flying down the track. *Please, Lord, keep me safe.* I don't know if it was my mind or my low back crying out for the finish line. *Whoosh!* I thought there were only fifteen turns on this course. *Whoosh!* Sliding through another.

Suddenly, it got very bumpy and jarring. Quickly, our speed reduced, and we skidded to a stop. My back pain eased; I breathed again. Wow, what a ride! Slowly, I climbed out of the sled, using the assistance offered, not knowing whether my back would support me or not.

Without a doubt, the most incredible ride of my life. Everyone was high-fiving one another, laughing, and smiling. I was putting on my best happy face. I had just checked off a bucket list item, but in all honesty, I was stunned. It was much more than I expected. Reaching nearly eighty miles per hour through the twists and turns.

Would I do it again? I don't know. However, I will watch it on the big screen with a new respect and tell everyone within earshot, "I've been there and done that!" Amazing.

Down the Slopes He Goes

Skiing is a wonderful activity, gliding downhill enjoying the beauty of the mountains, while getting quality exercise. It can be challenging; however, like many other things in life, if you want to be proficient, you must hit the slopes. I was preparing to test this hypothesis.

When my son graduated from high school, one of his gifts was to take a father-and-son ski trip once again. We decided to go in early to mid-December after his first college semester was finished but before the holiday season fully kicked off.

Plans were finalized for us to head to Park City, Utah. There are three ski resorts and others nearby; it was going to be a great week of skiing and hanging out together. After catching the resort shuttle, we arrived early enough to get our rental skis; we were ready to head out the next morning.

I had not skied in nearly ten years, put on twenty-plus pounds, but we were going skiing. A couple of green (easy) runs and we'd be ready to conquer the mountain. We caught the lift at the base of the mountain and headed up. My first ski maneuver would be getting off the lift and gliding out of the way of other skiers behind us. *Wham!* Off the lift, right onto my butt. Scrambling out of the way, then trying to stand on the slight incline. *Wham!* Back on my butt.

My mind was racing. *Come on, man, you're embarrassing yourself, get up!* Laughing, I tried making light of the situation. My son was just shaking his head. I had forgotten every lesson; it took me a long fall-filled thirty minutes to complete what should have been a five-minute run.

After arriving back at the base, I said we were both taking a ski class. Fortunately, because it was early in the season, we were the only ones assigned to our instructor. It was money well spent, and after just a few hours, I was gliding downhill like someone who had skied before. Not perfect—I fell getting off the lift again—but so much better, and if you're not falling, you're not pushing yourself (dad speak).

The first day on the mountain was rough, but the fundamentals were returning. A positive thing about the Park City area is that all the restaurants in town offering great food for any budget. One evening midweek, my son and I decided this was our day to splurge. Deer Valley Resort was well known for an evening seafood buffet. It is a high-end eating experience, but you get what you pay for—in this case, it was delicious food.

I cautioned my son to go slow, enjoy the buffet, and save room for dessert; they looked wonderful. It was an awesome dinner, I was full, but was debating whether to have a slice of cheesecake. After a couple of minutes, I decided to go for it. It was very good; I enjoyed every bite.

As we finished our meal and paid our check, I was hurting. I had overeaten. I told my son I needed to stroll for a minute in the cool night air before catching the shuttle back to our hotel. He called me, saying the shuttle was coming; I needed to walk, but he was insistent, saying it was cold. Climbing onto the bus, I was feeling somewhat better. We were sitting toward the back of the shuttle. Oh, this was a mistake. The bus was warm—no, it was *hot*—it was rocking side to side, frequently stopping and going again. I needed to get off this bus.

I stood and pulled the cord, signaling to get off at the next shuttle stop. The door opened, I started down the exit steps, and my stomach exploded. The cool air felt good, but the true relief came from the emptying of my stomach. People on the bus were "Oh mying" and murmuring about the effects of alcohol. I just felt better. We walked down the street; I was quickly back to normal.

That's a rabbit hole I don't want to repeat. Let's stick to skiing, not après-ski activities.

After four good days on the mountains around Park City, we regained our ski legs. It was still early in the ski season; a lot of the runs weren't open as the snow base was still being built. A decision was made to take the early shuttle to Snowbird Resort and test our abilities on their slopes.

Snowbird appeared to be a "Let's go skiing" resort versus Park City, a destination resort. The lifts were already operating and soon we were whisked up the mountain. The terrain was great; we had a fun morning gliding downhill. After a late lunch, we decided to head to Hidden Peak at the top of the mountain. There was a long intermediate run called Chip's Run, where we could ski from the peak to the base. It would be a special way to close out our day.

Snowbird also had several runs closed because of the reduced snowpack. Additionally, at eleven thousand feet, wind kept any fresh snow blown away, leaving very icy slopes. Hopping off the lift, we were ready to take the long cruise to the bottom of the mountain.

Somehow, we missed the turnoff and signage marking the way to Chip's Run. Now a couple hundred yards down the run, we had nothing but black diamonds in front of us, indicating expert skills required. We looked and debated; we had really been skiing well, handling many intermediate runs. The afternoon sun was shaded by the mountain; I could see the ice on the upper face of the trail.

It was steep; I told my son we would take long traverses until we cleared the first part of the run. I will go first, and you follow; we'll take our time and be fine. I eased onto the run and hadn't gone fifteen or twenty feet when I crossed a patch of ice, lost my balance, was on my back, and out of control.

The slope was steep; I couldn't stop, I was gaining speed, I could do nothing but go with the flow. I tried to shift and lift my legs so I wouldn't lose a ski. When I adjusted myself, I began to turn, no, I was spinning, but remaining on my back. There was no stopping me at this point; I was going faster, the steep icy track propelling me down the slope.

My slide was in slow motion in my mind, but being out of control, I couldn't tell how far I'd gone. Suddenly, I began to bounce; there were small moguls in my path, and I was no longer gliding but getting air and slamming back onto the frozen trail. For the first time, I became scared; I couldn't allow my head to bang against the ground. *"Lord, help me! Please help me!"*

The run leveled out, and I skidded to a stop. I moved my legs, then my arms, then I just lay still. I was giving thanks because nothing was particularly painful. "Thank You, Lord." While I lay motionless, others were springing into action.

Two members of the ski patrol were on the lift, saw me go down, and couldn't believe what they were watching. The first man arrived, spraying snow as he stopped.

"Are you okay?" he yelled at me.

"Yes," I said, sitting up and snapping back into reality.

Seeing I appeared uninjured, he let me have it. "What in hell are you thinking!" he said, not easing up. "You could have killed yourself!"

Suddenly, I remembered my son was at the top of the run, stammering, "My son is still uphill." The patrolman, toning it down, pointed, saying his partner was with him and would get him down. After again asking if I was okay, he called his partner to assure my son I was not injured.

Looking back up the slope, I could see them methodically making their way downhill. The patrolman once again said he hadn't seen a spill like that in a long time and that they had activated emergency rescue. He was glad I was okay, but he emphasized he wanted me off the mountain unless I was on a beginner run.

My son made it down the run to us, was visibly upset, but we enjoyed a very long hug. I had slid, spun, and bounced well over two hundred yards. On the positive side, the steepest part of the run was behind us. We said thank-you to the ski patrol; they left, telling us to be safe.

After a few minutes reviewing what had just happened, we headed downhill. We were in no rush; the skiing was easy, and the relaxation helped both of us put the incredible moment behind us. Arriving at the base, we decided to call it a day. It wasn't long before we climbed aboard the shuttle returning to Park City.

We spent our final day skiing at Park City. It was a fun day; fresh snow overnight had the slopes calling for us to ski. I had gained a new respect for the mountains, the beauty of snow-blanketed trees, continually reminding me that the good Lord was able and had watched over me once again.

The Rest of the Story

My family skied together several times after this trip. Attending ski school when needed, remembering our abilities, respecting the mountains and their Creator.

Snow skiing is great fun and is best done with family.

A HART EUROPEAN VACATION

Our family has strong Irish roots through both my mother and father. As children we always wore green on Saint Patrick's Day, in large part to avoid the pinches. On occasions when family history was discussed, the maternal side of Dad's family came to the United States through Ellis Island. Likewise, the maternal side of Mom's family entered through the Port of Savannah. Paternal sides also migrated from Ireland and Scotland. It was only natural to have the Emerald Isle on my travel bucket list.

We waited till my daughters were old enough to remember the trip. What age would that be? I decided the summer they were twelve and thirteen. My mother truly enjoyed traveling, had joined us on other trips, so she would be a great fit too. The four of us secured our passports, planned our route, and I added a couple of secret surprises. When the calendar turned to June, we were excited, anxious, and headed to the airport. The trip was no longer a dream; it was upon us, it was time to fly.

Remember to Drive on the Left

We flew overnight from Miami to Dublin via a connection in London. We were tired but it was still morning, so we picked up our rental car and we were off. All of us were focused.

"Dad, drive on the left side of the road."

"Ron, they drive differently here."

"Of course, it was already running through my mind, pay attention."

We didn't have GPS to assist, we were going old school, reading the map. I had already studied street maps, highlighted our route; we were out of the airport, headed to our first stop, Powerscourt Estate and Gardens. It was a great kickoff for our adventure: palatial house, a variety of manicured gardens, ponds, fountains, and sculptures.

Our twelve-day Irish journey had us staying in bed-and-breakfast homes nearly every night, and most of them were in the countryside. Our first night was no exception, arriving late afternoon; we were treated to tea and biscuits. It was enjoyable to relax, talk with the host, and learn about the area.

After tea, checking in, and having a dinner recommendation from our hostess, it was time to head into town, enjoy a meal, and return for a good night's sleep. Everyone was onboard and looking forward to, most of all, going to bed.

We pulled out onto the narrow two-lane country road. I naturally moved into the right-hand lane. We were all relaxed and enjoying watching the sheep in the green pastures. We had traveled about a mile when I noticed a vehicle approaching, but the car was in our lane. I remember flashing my lights, saying under my breath, "Hey, buddy, you're in my lane."

I began to brake, slowing down, then startling everyone, "What is this guy doing?"

Thankfully, the other car was also slowing. Suddenly, it hit me. "RON, YOU ARE IN THE WRONG LANE!"

I whipped our SUV over to the left lane. We passed one another at a near stop, with the driver glaring at us and me waving meekly.

I assume he was thinking, *Tourist season is back.* I was grateful he recognized the situation and slowed. Yes, it was a near miss, but it served as a wake-up call. Lesson learned, never again on the trip did I drive on the wrong side of the road.

Please Don't Predict Anything Else

Our journey was off to a wonderful start; the country is beautiful, the people friendly and helpful. We visited castles, both old and those still in use, primarily following the coastline as we circumnavigated the country. Around nearly every turn or rolling hill, we saw another amazing view.

We made stops at the Waterford Crystal Factory and the Rock of Cashel, an incredible ancient complex, elevated above the surrounding countryside. Then, we walked among cattle, getting a different perspective from nearby Hore Abbey.

Dangled over the edge of Blarney Castle's upper bulwark to kiss the Blarney Stone. Drove the Ring of Kerry, taking in all the views. None were any better than those from the Cliffs of Moher, upsetting my family when I stepped over the barrier wall to obtain and be in the perfect picture. Neither occurred, but I've been chastised forever; I still hear about it.

However, a disconcerting pattern was developing. As previously noted, we stayed in bed-and-breakfast lodgings throughout our trip. To be clear, four of us were in our party: Mom, a young seventy-four years old; my daughters, twelve and thirteen; and myself, a robust fifty.

We set our sleeping arrangements so one daughter slept in Dad's room and the other slept in Granny's room. Invariably, the host or hostess, showing us to our rooms, would turn and say to me, "You and the missus can stay in this room, and the children can stay over here."

"Excuse me! This is my mother," I would reply, while they would just smile and nod. Mom enjoyed the fun and smiled too.

The truth be known, I was developing some white areas in my red beard. The morning after I returned home, the beard came off. "Really, she is my mom! How old must I look?"

I need to refocus. We traveled out on the Dingle Peninsula, drove the Slea Head Scenic Drive, twenty-six miles of one extraordinary vista after another. Stopped to visit the 1,200-year-old Gallus Oratory, a small chapel and remarkable rock structure.

While at the small visitor's center, we picked up some snacks, including some nice-looking taffy. While driving away from the parking lot, Mom proclaimed, "This stuff could pull a tooth out of your head!" As we all laughed, moments later, "Oh no!" The taffy did just that, pulling a crown off its mooring in my mouth.

Beware, not only of the taffy on the Dingle Peninsula, but also, the first language and the road signs were in the Gaelic language, all adding to our adventure.

Now, One More Time

As we continued our journey around the Emerald Isle, we visited Kylemore Abbey, whose reflection in the lake it faces is the focus of many pictures. We crossed over into Northern Ireland where our sense of balance was tested as we scrambled across the geometric formations of the Giant's Causeway. Our fear of heights was triggered at Carrick-A-Rede Rope Bridge. Don't look down! There are unique and stunning locations all around this incredible island.

Another Northern Ireland highlight was a visit to Mussenden Temple, built originally as a library, completed in 1783. The circular edifice sits on a 120-foot cliff overlooking a wide sandy beach with the Atlantic Ocean waves breaking onto it. The views were something to behold, but the adventure for my daughters and Mom was crossing the sheep pasture to reach the library. The sheep were milling around the rolling green field, oblivious to the scenery; however, the healthy grass induced large amounts of sheep poop. It was an awkward dance watching them cross the pasture. Let's keep those new sneakers clean!

Midway through our Irish journey, it was time to spill the secrets I had been keeping from the family. It was early afternoon when I told everyone to help me find our next stop, Abbeyglen Castle; it must be close, but I hadn't seen any signs. A few minutes later, with their assistance, I turned our car into Abbeyglen Castle. However, I raised my family's eyebrows as we drove to the front of the castle. I informed them we would be staying here for the night.

"In a castle!" both girls exclaimed.

"Yes," I explained, "it's Granny's birthday!"

We had reservations for dinner, but we had a few hours, so I hastily washed some underwear, hanging them to dry in a back window. My daughter was totally embarrassed, saying I was so wrong.

"This is a castle." She still reminds me of this when we reflect on the trip (but I did it again a few days later in Dublin).

After visiting the ruins of an ancient castle, we returned to our castle. I told everyone to dress up for supper because we are dining here at the castle. It was the most formal evening of our journey. There were flower-decorated candlestick holders on the tables as centerpieces, but they elevated the candles, so they didn't obstruct our vision while at the table. We were seated near the center of the room.

As we finished a delicious meal, the table was cleared, the maître d' came over, speaking quietly to me. I nodded yes, he smiled, affirming by patting my shoulder.

As the girls and Mom were discussing dessert options, the lights dimmed, and the wait staff waltzed in carrying a large round birthday cake complete with sparklers, candles, and an American flag. It seemed the entire restaurant was watching. The maître d' called on everyone to sing "Happy Birthday" to Eloise.

After a routine singing, the maître d' implored the diners, "Sing it again, only this time like you mean it!" This led to a robust singing of "Happy Birthday." The girls were thrilled, Mom was joyously taking it all in. It was perfect, and fittingly, it took place in a castle. So proud of her! Happy seventy-fourth, Mom.

The Rest of the Story

All birthdays should include surprises and a gift. Well, the surprise was wonderful, but as we enjoyed the cake, I asked the girls what gift we had for Granny. Of course, being in the middle of our journey, they gave an oops look, but I told them I had them covered. "Granny just wants your love and a big hug." However, when we go to London next week, we are going to take a day trip on the Eurostar Train to Paris. This was met with joy and excitement, especially from Mom.

Our journey in Ireland was spectacular, we did visit Belfast, Mount Stewart House and Gardens, and finished with couple of nights in Dublin. The city, like the countryside, was full of surprises, cathedrals, Guinness Brewery, a picture with Molly Malone, Grafton Street, and even a duck boat tour. However, after more than ten days away from the States, my daughters requested dinner at Captain America's—not once but back-to-back nights.

This was a European adventure, so although I loved being in Ireland, we were headed to London and Paris.

Excitement on the Tube

We arrived in London and the tenor of our journey changed. Not only were we in a big city, instead of vistas and scenery, we were inundated with history. It seemed everywhere we looked, there was another site from schoolbooks, novels read, or the nightly news. Our hotel was next to the London Eye. Close to so much, we were ready to explore.

We hit the ground running: the Tower of London, Tower Bridge, Saint Peter's, Big Ben, Parliament, Buckingham Palace, took a ride on the Eye, attended Evensong at Westminster Abbey seated in the choir loft, spent hours at Kew Gardens, and visited several museums.

So many sites were close at hand, but to best get around London, you ride the Tube (the name of their subway system). It is efficient, easy to use, and runs on time. Being from South Florida, we were newbies at using the Tube, but not for long.

One afternoon, we headed down the runway to reach the subway platform. A train was already in the station with its doors open, welcoming riders. I said this might be our train, while I was looking for the route name on the train, my thirteen-year-old daughter bounced into the car. Then the doors closed, three of us on the platform, and my daughter with the most bewildered look on her face on the train. Hands on each side of her face, literally like a scene out of *Home Alone*, as the car began to pull away, I yelled to her to get off at the next stop; she nodded okay.

As she rode out of sight into the subway tunnel, my mind was racing. I couldn't think, Mom and younger daughter stunned, not believing what just happened. Where is the next train? It couldn't arrive soon enough. Mom was quiet, but I know looking back, she was praying.

I paced back and forth, trying to recall what just happened, beating myself up, how did this occur! Finally, the next train arrived; we didn't hesitate, the doors opened, we were in the car. Feeling some relief, we were just moments from reuniting. Thankfully, we were starting down the tracks, just one stop.

As we were pulling into the next station, I began looking for my daughter on the platform out of the windows; I didn't see her. We stopped, and I bounded out of the car, looking everywhere on the platform. No daughter! Where was my daughter! Her sister began crying loudly.

I'm in another country; I've lost my daughter! Did she not hear me? Is she still on the train? I don't know the area and neither does she! For the first time, what else could have happened crossed my mind. *What did I do? What do I do now? Lord, I need help!*

Looking down the platform once again, I see the hat of a bobby, a London policeman. *Maybe he can help. I hope so!* The three of us approached the policeman. I blurt out my story, sister crying louder.

He said, "Relax, and let's go up toward the station office."

He spoke to a woman in the office. I assured my youngest daughter things will be alright. The lady asks what station we arrived from and verifies that my missing daughter was on the previous train from that station. "Yes, yes," I reply, trying to be calm. She looks again at her station chart. Looking up, she knows we are hurting, but she informs us my daughter's train departed the station and went to the left, the train we took goes straight and veers to the right.

That possibility had never crossed my mind. We went in different directions! I was speechless.

Before I could gather myself to start screaming about losing my daughter, another person in the office called to her, getting her attention. A young girl had gone to a station office saying she had lost her family. What!

They verified our names and asked a couple of questions to confirm who we were. Then the policeman walked us out of the station, told us to walk about four hundred yards straight down the street, and we would see the station where my daughter was. "Take care and enjoy London," he said.

We walked as quickly as possible down the busy sidewalk. Reaching the station office, we shared tears of joy and the best hugs from all of us.

The other part of the story: When the next train arrived, and we weren't on it, my daughter had gone to a Tube employee. She explained her situation and was taken to the station office.

There were lots of thanks given that afternoon, evening, and for years afterward.

Intrigue on the Tower

On our third full day in London, we were ticketed to take the Eurostar Train to Paris. We were up early in the morning; our hotel was near the train station, walking to the station we were more excited with each step to be headed to "The City of Light."

Following our three-hour train ride, we had arrived in Paris, France. It was mid-morning and time to get started. We caught an off-and-on sightseeing bus outside the train station. Each of us was eager to see the sights on a beautiful early summer day, we pointed and were awed as we rode down the Champs Elysée. We rounded the Arc de Triomphe, passed the Louvre Museum, and Cathedrale Notre Dame with its gargoyles looking down at us.

We took a boat ride on the River Seine, which gave us a different perspective of all the amazing architecture we had been viewing. It was quite nice and a change of pace.

The Eiffel Tower stood above the entire scene of palaces, river, cathedrals, gardens, museums, and open malls. We had seen and photographed it from so many angles, the only remaining adventure was to go to the top.

We got in line, tickets in hand, and soon we were on the elevator heading to the upper viewing platforms. Announcements played in various languages, discussing the tower, then warned us to beware of pickpockets. I instructed the girls to stay close and keep their eyes open.

The upper viewing area consists of two levels joined by stairs. The lower is closed in with glass windows, but on the fenced upper level, it is open for breathtaking breezy vistas and photography.

The viewing area is over nine hundred feet above the bustling city below. We bought some French pastries and drinks as we relaxed and took in the view. The pastries were not up to French standards, but being at the top of the Eiffel Tower on a clear, calm day was awesome.

I looked around and realized my twelve-year-old daughter was not with us. My heart sank as I looked around the platform; where was she? The area is a square, each side just over fifty feet long. I told my mother and other daughter to stay put as I sought her.

My mind was blank, scurrying around the area! I had just done this two days before in London. *O Lord, not again!* In a foreign country, and English is not the primary language!

I told Mom I was going down to the lower level. Hustling down the stairs, eyes searching in all directions. The lower level has the same dimensions but has obstructed views to look across the platform. I was trying to hurry, but not be rude. *I need to find my daughter! Lord, I need you!*

The elevator message filled my head, "Danger! Beware! We told you!"

Then rounding another corner, there she was! I stopped; she was just slowly walking, looking at the expansive city below, totally unaware we thought she was lost. I gathered myself, gave thanks, walked over, giving her a big hug. Staying calm, which was nearly impossible, while she explained she was just looking out of the windows. I explained we were afraid she was lost, we needed to get back to the upper floor and stay together.

As we climbed the staircase, she saw Granny and her sister and realized everyone was shaken by her actions. Once again, hugs all around and more than a few "Thank You, Jesuses" were said. I just sat for a few minutes, told the others to take a final look, but I needed to be still.

The day in Paris was wonderful, we were introduced to a magnificent city. All of us agreed we would have to come back and truly explore the city properly. As the day wound down, we took the sightseeing bus back to the train station. We made just one stop at an

American Bar-B-Que restaurant. We were in a city known for great food, and we found some.

I must add the Eurostar Train System was special, a very smooth ride. I worked many years in a busy industrial railyard with clanging jointed rail, speeds under ten miles per hour, and a few derailments a year. When it was announced, we were traveling at 186 miles per hour, I just tightened my seatbelt and pretended not to hear.

The Rest of the Story

Our European vacation was incredible, I still look at pictures of the trip and smile. So many memories. Oh, there were a couple of bumps in the road, but we learned more about one another, our heritage, other cultures, witnessed God's creative handiwork, and some special man-made architecture too.

Till this day I remain thankful the Lord watched over my family when most needed.

IT MUST BE CHRISTMAS

I can't write a story about the chapters of my life without talking about Christmas. It has always been the best day of the year. As a youngster, it was all about the anticipation of the big day and the gifts.

The decorated tree in the house was the focal point. There was never a hint of gifts, but on Christmas morning the area under and around the tree was full of presents. Dad would have the eight-millimeter movie camera on, its lights blinding us as we ran into the room, Looking around in awe then grabbing our stockings and finding a place to sit down.

Mom and Dad didn't have a lot, but as kids, we thought we were the luckiest children around. Each shirt or pair of pants came in their own box, so it seemed like more. Our stockings always had a few pieces of candy, but a new toothbrush also. There was one special unique gift for each of us six kids.

Beneath the tree, I discovered my first train set, riding the rails in a large circle. One year a roller coaster ride was set up in the room, sending us screaming down the hallway. A unicycle on another; I never mastered it, but took some awesome falls, receiving scrapes and bruises.

After Dad retired from the Navy, Christmas Eve was Grandparent's Night; we would go to their home for supper and exchange gifts with them. Granny and Granddaddy were great people, hard workers; their outlook on life and wisdom impacted all our lives. Christmas Eve set the tone that amplified as the big day drew closer. We always got one gift from Mom and Dad too, which was new pajamas to wear that night and have on for Christmas morning.

Then as a teenager, it became more about gifts, family, and food. As I started working farmer's fields, earning a few dollars, giving to others became part of the day. Learning the very true lesson, it's better to give than receive. One year I received a Polaroid camera, setting me up for a lifetime of joy through photography.

The constant theme of Christmas at home was the birth of Christ and understanding the true meaning of Christmas. Dad would always read the verses from Luke chapter two from his King James Version of the Bible. Jesus born humbly in a stable is the greatest gift of all.

In my midtwenties, I was out of the country three straight years, far from home with limited communication. Suddenly the song "I'll be home for Christmas" had a deeper meaning. I attended Noche Buena dinners, midnight Mass at the main basilica in Maracaibo, and caroling in Maracay. We even put a string of miniature lights on the hotel wall in the shape of a Christmas tree. It wasn't home, especially when single, waking up with no family to celebrate with. However, Christmas was always a remarkable day.

As a dad, I tried to teach and show my children the importance of love, family, giving, and the true reason for the holiday. Baking cookies with my children for neighbors and special friends. Attending school and church programs. Taking plenty of pictures, thankful for the "I love you Daddys."

Now, as granddaddy the day remains very special. Cherishing the moment the boys run into the room, faces full of awe; the wonder is always there. The morning they were excitedly bouncing when their heads banged together, gashing an eyebrow. We still smile when seeing pictures of the patched-up brow. I have the privilege of reading the Christmas story in Luke. I use my father's well-read bible.

I could tell of blessings and Christmas stories all day, but one story stands apart.

When Santa Swore

The term *holiday season* was very true in the Hart household as we grew up. The house was decorated inside and out, special decorations came out of closets and were set up on display.

Christmas music, both carols and songs, filled the air for weeks ahead of the big day. Bing Crosby's voice echoed through the house, seemingly never-ending. From "Dominick the Donkey" to "It's Christmas at Our House" with its appropriate wording, "The door is open, don't knock just come inside."

However, the hands-down favorite sing-along was "Sisters," starting with the first note from the Andrew Sisters. My four sisters were singing, dancing, and going through the routine from the movie *White Christmas*. Now sixty years later, they still belt it out together starting in October; no, it doesn't sound any better!

While my dad was stationed in Norfolk, Virginia, it was decided we would travel to Florida and celebrate Christmas with our grandparents. Everyone was excited, so when school was dismissed for the holidays, we climbed into the three-bench seat station wagon and headed south.

Not everyone in the family was feeling great. A stomach virus had made its way through the family. However, we were headed to Granny's, and it was going to be a fun time. They lived in Central Florida; the weather would be warm and welcoming.

It wasn't unusual for us to pack the station wagon and head to Granny's. We had taken trips from California, New York, and several times from Virginia. There were very few stops, and if needed, Dad would stop in a rest area for a few hours of sleep. Meals were normally sandwiches made during the drive by Mom. So when Dad said we were going to be stopping for dinner at a truck stop ahead, we were excited.

We piled around a table and a booster seat was brought over for my brother who was two and a half at the time. Much to our surprise, a Santa Claus was there, entertaining children while they waited for their meal. We were no different; all of us made our way to sit on Santa's knee except my brother.

Santa was determined to speak with all the children in the restaurant, so he walked over to our table to personally invite my brother but was rejected. Undaunted, he called several times for him to come sit on his knee.

Finally, my brother relented and walked over to speak with Santa. Mr. Claus was full of himself and was making sure everyone knew he had succeeded. "Who is this coming to see me?" Reaching down, picking him up, setting him on his knee. Santa started to slowly bounce his knee while asking, "Well, little boy, what do you want for Christmas?" No sooner were the words out of Santa's mouth when my brother leaned forward, vomiting onto Santa's chest.

"Ho, ho, ho!" quickly turned into "Oh no! No! No!" He whisked my brother back to our table, where Mom accepted him while apologizing. Santa then disappeared toward the restroom.

We were stunned. What just happened? My brother just puked on Santa Claus. His Christmas was surely done! Without it being said, Dad was telling us to finish up; we needed to hit the road. He and Mom were embarrassed; we kids wanted to laugh but knew better.

As we were wrapping up, I decided to make a trip to the bathroom. I walked in to see Santa by the sink trying to clean his suit. Then as I approached the urinal, I heard it. Santa was angrily muttering to himself, "That little son of a bitch!" Then again, "That little son of a bitch."

I froze, knowing he was talking about my brother. He continued his rant; I couldn't squeeze out a drop. Nothing was going to happen; I zipped up my zipper. Approach Santa at the sink? Not a chance! Santa was mad, wet, and swearing. A quick look, and I was out the door.

My brother felt much better after emptying his stomach. There were no further incidents, and Santa must have been forgiving, as Christmas gifts still came a few days later.

I love Christmas—by far my favorite holiday.

A MOST REMARKABLE LADY

How do I begin writing a story about the best mother I could ever have had? I knew from a young age she was special, but all moms are special, right?

On Mother's Day at church, it seemed she was always recognized "The Mother with the Most Children Present." All six of her children were always in church with her and Dad, so she was naturally going to win.

Then when I was about ten, the church decided to have a vote for the "Mother of the Year." Well, I voted for my mother and knew she was the shoo-in winner, as everyone would vote for their mother, and she had the most children. It was a slam dunk—go, Mom!

However, I began to hear people talking about voting for Ms. Eloise. That was my mother. But I was puzzled—why weren't they voting for their own mother? Slowly, I began to understand not everyone's mom was part of the church or may not be alive. I remember debating whether I need to campaign for my mom, because just having the most children wouldn't be enough.

Mother's Day finally arrived. Who was going to win? At last, the pastor stood to announce the vote. Before saying who, he said the winner was a good mother, loved the Lord, and was kind, caring, generous, and had a big heart. She received votes from young people, parents, and our mature members. Oh no, my friends and other young people voted for someone other than their mother, I was worried. Then the pastor said the "Mother of the Year is Eloise Hart." There was a lot of applause, including from my family.

This was probably the first time I began to understand how blessed I was to have my mom as my *mother*.

An Upbringing in Hardship

My mother was born in 1931, just as the Great Depression was taking hold. Her family, like so many others, was hit hard when the banks and the economy collapsed. Living in Florida on a small farm may have eased the pain, but the hardship was real. There are pictures of her early school classes; many of the students, including her, were barefoot.

Mom loved music; she didn't have the greatest voice, but she enjoyed singing. In high school, she was a member of the marching band. She was a majorette and could really twirl a baton, eventually becoming drum major. We attended several college football games together; while others headed to concessions at halftime, she was focused on the bands. While vacationing, I purchased a CD of hits from the forties; she knew all the songs, singing and humming along to the music. She loved singing hymns too, her favorite being "Just a Closer Walk with Thee."

Her parents never fully trusted the banks after their closing and all funds were lost. Through the years, Mom would save and hide money in her home. At one point in her eighties, she had $10,000 squirreled away.

Two things a difficult life couldn't take away were the love in their household and a strong belief in God. Her father passed away when she was in high school; but the love and caring between her mother, three brothers, and herself was a family model. Not perfect, but all hardworking, and they returned to live on or near the old homeplace. They all could be found in church on Sunday morning, thankful for God's grace and blessings.

Mom Being Mom

Mom enjoyed having a good time; she valued family gatherings. And keep your eyes open—she may be pulling a prank! Dad was the recipient of most of them.

We were on one of those long cross-country drives—Mom, Dad, and the six of us kids. A car started to pass our station wagon. When it slowed, the lady passenger was staring at our vehicle. Then with her finger raised, she began to count the number of children in the car. While we were looking back at her, Mom took a pillow and tucked it under her shirt. When the counter got alongside the front row, Mom waved and pointed at her now large-looking stomach. The woman's mouth fell open, then putting her hand over her mouth as the driver suddenly increased speed pulling away. Mom had the biggest laugh.

As youngsters, we started cooking Mother's Day breakfast to serve her in bed. As we entered her bedroom, she would act all surprised and happy. She always said Dad had to eat first, which he would, saying how good the food was. Years later, we learned the rest of the story. Mom would create a distraction, having us all look away momentarily, empty her plate under the covers, then acting as if she had a mouth full of food when we turned back around to her empty plate. Telling us how much she loved us and enjoyed the breakfast. It worked for years until we learned to actually cook well.

Mom was a terrific cook also. As the family moved around the country based on where Dad was stationed in the Navy, she would learn to cook local favorites. In Newport, she learned to make a wonderful New England clam chowder. In San Diego, she learned Mexican dishes; we ate tacos and other meals back on the east coast long before they were popular. Also, on the West Coast, she learned Asian cuisine, making delicious sweet-and-sour pork, chop suey, and chow mein.

Mom never saw color in people; she had friends of all backgrounds and raised us to do the same. I remember visiting my grandparents one summer and was at the Market Picnic. An annual town event featuring food, contests, and highlighted by the local electrical co-op raffle in the evening. I was about nine at the time and went to town to help Mom carry back plates of barbecue.

While walking through the market area set up for the raffle, I noticed rows of benches, but at the back, crates were stacked for seating, and the word *spooks* was written on them in several places.

So I asked Mom, "What are spooks?"

She promptly sat me down, firmly saying, "That is what some people call black people. But it is wrong, and I better never hear you speak that way, or I'll wash your mouth out with soap!"

Many times, people of color stopped by the house just to talk. Mom and Dad always welcomed them. When Mom reflected on her childhood, she would say it took the entire community to make it through the tough times. She knew the parents and grandparents of most local visitors.

Mom had strong friendships for decades that sustained both parties in good and bad times. My daughters and I met with Mom and one of her friends she hadn't seen in over twenty years. We talked and shared over lunch, but then the two ladies walked to a quiet place, hugged, and just sat together. They had carried each other through dark times; I saw the definition of friendship defined in them.

Mom could cook, bake, and keep a spotless house as well as anyone. However, don't think she was a softy. She was tough, and you'd better listen the first time. She could slip off a shoe, whack me on the bottom while holding a younger sibling without batting an eye. Additionally, she had Dad as powerful backup, and none of us wanted to go there.

When Dad retired from active duty in the Navy, funds were tight. With most of us kids in school, Mom began to work at the elementary school cafeteria. She was the dishwasher and clean-up person. In time, her work ethic moved her to school cafeteria manager, hands down serving the best meals in the county for more than twenty-plus years.

I don't know what it was that planted the travel bug inside Mom. Maybe it was the cross-country trips in the station wagon or seeing our country's beauty while Dad was stationed in various cities. Whatever it was, she was always ready to go. When they both retired for good, they purchased an RV and began traveling around the country, frequently meeting up with former veteran groups.

They were on the road when Dad suffered a life-ending heart attack. He was only sixty-eight years old, had just passed his annual physical. Mom and Dad were finally living their dream life: six successful children, several grandchildren, healthy, a paid-for dream home just a few years old, and the ability to hit the road.

Mom's life was shattered as the love of her life and forty-five years of marriage ended so unexpectedly. Just eight months later, it was Mom in the hospital with health issues. Visiting the hospital was one of the hardest things in my life. Here was the person who always cared for me as a sick child and encouraged me throughout my life, lying in the bed. I couldn't deal with it.

She was still heartbroken over Dad's passing; I truly believe she had to decide whether to pass on or go forward for her children and grandchildren. The latter happened, and she lived another twenty-three active years, being a wonderful mother and granny. Having a positive impact on each of our lives. Thank You, Jesus.

The most important thing I learned from my mother, after the importance of faith, was to value others. Starting with family, friends, coworkers, and those you meet.

The Queen of Christmas

During the recent holiday season, I heard several conversations about who was the queen of Christmas? Anyone growing up in my family or living in the area knew hands down it was my mother. When you talk about the big day, she checked all the boxes.

The decorations began coming out of the closet or utility shed just after Thanksgiving. Our home was transformed, especially the family room. The tree would be set up there along with knickknacks, many older than us. Two huge white pine tree cones were set out on the dining room hutch and decorated like miniature Christmas trees. They are now over sixty-five years old.

Her last two homes had a brick wall in the family room along with a fireplace or Franklin stove. Stockings were sewn by Mom out of used fabric. Then with all the grandchildren, she sewed new stockings for everyone. The empty stockings were hung by the fireplace, hoping on Christmas morning they would be filled. Mom never made or hung a stocking for herself. As we became adults, a long pink sock was hung for her.

The stereo record player was always nearby awaiting Bing Crosby to begin singing.

The family room may have been the focal point of decorations. However, the kitchen was a place full of wondrous smells; cookies, cakes, pies, and lots of candies. Mom always made a mincemeat pie for Dad, an applesauce cake (my favorite), the fruitcakes made months ahead with daughters were unwrapped and ready to serve.

As kids, mom sewed all of us new pajamas for the big morning. Nobody slept in on Christmas morning, but we understood the rules. Mom and Dad checked the family room before anyone entered.

After the chaos of opening our gifts and a quick breakfast, we would all settle down while Dad read the Christmas story, a reminder of how blessed we were.

One year a family of friends from Argentina visited at Christmas, one of the children was twelve at the time. They were in awe of the celebration, from the decorations, food, gifts, and family love. I was in Buenos Aires forty years later, the young girl, now a mother with her own family, said hands down Christmas at Mom's was the best holiday experience ever.

A Woman of Faith

I've written things about how special Mom was—they are all true. However, don't get the idea that her life was easy and that things just fell in place for her.

Already mentioned was her father's passing when she was in high school, my dad's death at sixty-eight, just when retirement was looking promising. Those weren't the only tragedies in her life.

When I was one, my older sisters were two and three. One afternoon they got into orange-flavored baby aspirin. Thinking it was candy, they chewed and enjoyed many of them. I didn't get to participate because I couldn't get out of my crib, and they didn't share. Mom found the girls not feeling well and realized what had happened.

She called Dad at work, then yelling for help from the friend mentioned earlier, she and her friend rushed the girls to the emergency room. Their stomachs were pumped and flushed. After many hours, they were both released to go home. The next morning, when Mom came in to wake the girls. Sharon had passed away.

Mom was eight months pregnant. Now her first child was taken from her. She broke down, her doctors concerned with her emotional state and pregnancy refused to allow her to attend most of the funeral services. She leaned on Dad, her mother, her good friend, and the Lord.

Later during the grieving process, she had a dream, seeing Sharon holding hands with a dear aunt on a walkway in a beautiful lakeside garden surrounded by blooming flowerbeds. Her aunt told her Sharon was okay, well taken care of, and they would meet again. Now she had her life to live, and her family needed her.

Mom did live a full life; Sharon was always in her heart. Of her seven children, only Sharon and her daughter born a month later were red-haired.

Always the encourager, Mom served the Lord in many ways. She was active in her Sunday school class, missions, and leading the Girls Auxiliary (GAs), which was taught in our home. Throughout her life hospitality was front and center, potlucks, meals for others in need, setting up, cleanup, or just having others over for meals.

She loved children. You would think with seven of her own she may back away from volunteering in the nursery. But she embraced it from her early days as a parent till well into her seventies. Her special talent was the "La La Song"—she would rock children and quietly sing "La la…" over and over. In doing so, even the most rambunctious child would be asleep in minutes. I remember my nephew reaching up telling her "No! Stop singing 'la la,'" knowing he would soon be sleeping.

She had a forgiving heart. I know people who said, wrote, or did things that hurt her deeply. It would wound her; but somehow, with the Lord's assistance, she would work her way through it. Giving it away. Remarkably, I saw several of those people come to love and embrace her. Mom fully accepted them never mentioning past grievances.

My mother and father were people of prayer. Every night they would get on their knees side by side next to their bed and pray. You may say what a model for each of us kids, indeed it was. However, they prayed for each of us by name, if we were having a bad attitude day, a problem with a sibling, or trouble in school they were calling on the Lord for help. When you are a child or teenager, you don't necessarily want to hear a recap of your day. When we went to bed we wanted to go sleep.

Even when I was on vacation, I received plenty of work phone calls because of my position. One day when I was about sixty, I was at my mom's, and we were getting ready to have lunch. Work called, it was a frustrating discussion, problems with the railway and customers. After hanging up, I was wound up, so I asked Mom to say the blessing before we ate.

She began to pray; her voice was soft but strong. She was speaking to her Lord, there was no routine blessing said before every meal. She prayed from her heart, simple, pure, and thankful. Mentioning the food, me, family, and a couple of special requests on her heart.

I was humbled, I'd been praying for a good portion of my life, with some results too. However, she went straight to the throne room to say grace for an ordinary lunch. When you stop, remember who you're speaking with and believe, it makes a difference.

*****

I called her "A Most Remarkable Lady" to start this story. She truly was, and I got to call her *Mom*.

The Rest of the Story

When Dad retired and moved south, I was introduced to Spanish moss. It looks nice hanging in the trees, gently waving in a breeze. However, it does fall off branches and after a storm can cover the yard. Then it was my chore for years to clean the yard picking up the moss.

In South Florida suburbs, we don't have much Spanish moss. When an oak tree was planted in front of my home, some of the moss picked up in my mom's yard made its way into my oak. It now hangs long, low and aggravates some getting in and out of their cars. For me it's a reminder of home and a special lady.

THE LONGEST 24

It was late in the month of June 2008 when the unexpected happened. I had just returned from a wonderful family vacation. Four of my five siblings and their families had gathered at my sister's home in Wyoming to celebrate family and our mother's birthday. Afterward, my daughters, mom, and I extended our time out west and spent another ten days enjoying the beauty of our country. This story starts with the preparations for this adventure.

One of the most important parts of a great vacation is the homework and scheduling done ahead of time. For me, this was exciting stuff I enjoy doing. In booking part of the trip, I was asked a key question: How much do you weigh?

We visited Yellowstone, the Tetons, Arches, Grand Canyon, Zion, and Bryce Canyon National Parks along the way, with many other incredible stops. No, it wasn't river rafting who asked the question; it was for a mule ride at Bryce Canyon.

Yep, the mule riders needed to know how much each of us weighed. Why? Because there was a weight limit, 220 pounds. This mule ride was going to get me in trouble twice. The next time I visited Publix grocery store, the scale read 235 pounds. "Big boy." I had two months—shouldn't be any problem. I started walking in the evening, eating salads, and tried avoiding the pastries always showing up at work. This effort would make a big difference shortly. Yes, I made weight.

I must share the second part of the mule ride trouble. As noted in the first paragraph, we celebrated Mom's seventy-seventh birthday.

When we arrived at our hotel outside of Bryce Canyon, I went over the plans for the next day. "The girls and I are going on a mule ride early tomorrow—"

"EXCUSE ME!" Mom protested. "I rode our family mule frequently when I was growing up [yes, there are pictures]. Why can't I ride?"

The girls and I had been on horse trail rides at least three times while on vacation with Mom. She always waited for us at the hotel, *but* this struck home. She was ready to show us how to ride a mule; after all, the old family mule was also blind. Well, she didn't join us on for the ride, but I was in the doghouse for a while.

It's also important to note we did some walks together in some parks. For longer hikes, my oldest daughter and I tackled the trails, while Mom and my younger daughter would visit the visitor center or the downtown areas of the quaint towns. I distinctly remember it was ninety-five degrees at 5:00 p.m. when we headed out on the three-mile moderately strenuous trail to Delicate Arch in Arches National Park. There was a lot of resting and water breaks on this stroll, but it was amazing and worth the effort.

We completed our big loop journey back at my sister's Wyoming home. Then it was time to say goodbye and fly home. We landed in Orlando, got Mom home, leaving the girls south of Orlando for extended vacation time with their mother.

A day after returning home from the wondrous west, I was back at work. Two external company trucks collided with each other in our yard just after lunchtime. While investigating the accident with the safety manager, it seemed to be so hot. I was telling him about hiking in all the high temperatures, but I didn't sweat like this. Water seemed to be pouring out of me; thankfully, I had a change of clothes in the office and plenty of water to hydrate. Welcome back to Florida's humidity.

After work, I stopped at Taco Bell on the way home to pick up supper. My friend and coworker Tony laughed later in the evening, saying I needed to eat better, but it was easy, filling, and no line in the drive-through.

Once home, I unlaced and kicked off my heavy steel-toed work boots and enjoyed my dinner. It was quiet with everyone out, but the cat seemed to appreciate having me back at home. During my meal, I was thinking, I should continue my evening walks. My weight was down a little, maybe; I ate well on vacation. It wasn't going to hurt anything, so finish and hit the sidewalk.

I slipped into my sneakers, walked out of the community, and onto the wide sidewalks along Johnson Street. It was just after seven in the evening, and the temperature had begun dropping, and there was a light breeze, a great time for a stroll.

The sidewalk on the north side of Johnson Street has curves, passes a couple of lakes, interrupted by two communities. There are trees which furnish a little shade but primarily add to a relaxed view. I wasn't looking into the Grand Canyon or strolling past Balancing Rock as I was a week earlier, but it is an easy, peaceful walk. It was good to be home.

Just over a mile into the trek, I was feeling good, so I extended my original plans and walked further east. Reaching a turn-around point, I crossed over the street to return on the south side of the street. The sidewalk here is fairly straight and follows a lake nearly all the way back to my community. Getting exercise, drifting off, and relaxing all at the same time.

Just as I passed the end of the lake, wow, I got tired. Come on Ron, you can't be whipped already; it's just over a quarter mile back to the house. I was just hiking in our national parks, but Florida took me down on my first walk back home. I was exhausted, thankfully there was a bus bench, and I parked myself on it. What's going on? I'm only about three miles along, and bam, I'm done.

After sitting for about five minutes, I began feeling better. The breeze definitely felt good, I got up, walking uneventfully back to the house. Boy, that was strange.

Back at the house, I took a long shower, did a few things around the house, checked in with the guys at work, and watched a little TV. For three weeks, I had barely watched any TV, much better things to do.

However, something in my head kept saying, "Ron, something isn't right."

I argued back, "I feel fine."

This running battle continued as I slipped into bed. It was normal bedtime somewhere—nine thirty to ten o'clock. The voice in my head was still yapping, "Hey, the hospital is only a quarter mile away," to which I would respond, "I'm fine, talk to me in the morning."

But finally, the voice used the trump card. "Think about your kids. It doesn't hurt to get checked out."

I couldn't fight back, "Why did you say that, bringing the kids into the fray?" I got dressed for a quick trip to the emergency room.

I made two calls as I headed to the ER: one to my boss, leaving a message saying I was fine but driving to the hospital to confirm it, and the other to my son, telling him not to come; I'd keep him in the loop. He lived twenty-five minutes away, and I could be back home by the time he drove up. My boss called back, fussing at me not to drive but to call 911. I responded, "Please, I'm a quarter mile from the hospital, am already there, and will update him."

Walking into the ER, I took a quick look around. "Great! They don't look very busy. I'll be out of here soon."

"Sir, why are you here? Can we help you?" asks the receptionist.

"I'm feeling okay, but I think something may be wrong," I replied to a puzzled look.

"Give me your name and take a seat." I had just broken every rule of triage. If you want to be seen in an ER, you'd better have an issue.

It wasn't all that long before, "Ronald, come on back."

"So what's going on, sir?" I explained what happened when I walked and that I still don't feel quite right but can't put a finger on why. "Well, let's see what we can find out."

Blood pressure? "Good." Temperature? "Good." Pulse? "Good." Blood oxygen level? "Good."

"We are going to do a precautionary EKG, so hang tight for a minute, then we'll get you out of here."

A team of two guys stopped by and hooked me up to the machine. It wasn't long before one nudged the other to get his attention while pointing at the machine. Almost at the same time, they asked firmly in unison, "Are you feeling okay?"

I calmly responded, "Yes, I feel okay."

Then they dropped the bomb. *"Sir, you are having a heart attack right now."*

I said, "What, really!"

They said, "We must get you to a room."

I said okay as I stood to walk with them. They shouted, "Sit down!" then the drama started.

"Code blue! Code blue!" was announced in the sound system. A wheelchair was brought in, and I was whisked away toward a room where a couple of nurses were hurrying in to get me into the bed and put me in a gown. It was just like I was on TV.

I felt like I was in a circus with all the activity around me, but I didn't know what the next step would be. Then I made the second good decision (the first being listening to my body), a doctor strolled in carrying a huge syringe with a needle I wanted no part of... It looked like one's we used to give cows shots when I was growing up.

"What is that?" I questioned, nearly shouting in fear.

"Are you in any pain?" he asked.

"No, sir!" I replied. "I feel fine, but apparently my heart doesn't agree."

He asked again, but I assured him I wasn't hurting, as I shook my head no! I wanted no part of that needle. He said okay, but we'll keep it here in case we need it. Later, I asked the doctor what was in the syringe, and he replied morphine, which would have knocked me out and minimized my input to treatment for the evening.

Once that was settled, I had to call my son, telling him I was going to be admitted, as testing needed to be done. I asked him to come, but I didn't dare tell him why, as he would be driving a hundred miles an hour to get there. I also called back to my boss letting know I was having a heart attack, was being admitted, and testing would determine the next steps. However, I won't be at work tomorrow.

My son arrived and just as I was finished explaining what was happening, a team came in to take me up for an emergency angioplasty. The clock was pushing midnight, and I was in a medical "twilight" as the procedure started. I remember the staff talking and saying blockages were not something they could clear.

At this point three things were obvious to the doctors and nurses:

1. They now considered me critical and were expediting my care.
2. They needed to transfer me to a different hospital.
3. It was apparent to them, I would need heart bypass surgery, ASAP.

Thankfully my son was with me, I was awake and although now well medicated, I was able to talk with him about treatment going forward. It seemed every time I turned around there was a new IV to be inserted or pills to take.

The ambulance arrived; however, it wasn't to be a normal ride. A cardiac nurse was assigned to ride with us. A blood pump which was inserted in my groin to assist after the angioplasty stopped working on the trip, but I was just a chatterbox, embarrassing my son.

Oh, look! We're on Johnson Street. I was just walking there hours ago. I knew a recently retired captain with the city EMT / fire department. "Surely, you know my friend Jimmy?" They just nodded and were speeding along, while I just kept talking, telling stories nobody wanted to hear. Yep, medicines can be good.

The ambulance arrived at the hospital. The EMTs wished me well, probably glad I was out of the wagon. The hospital was expecting me and moved me quickly to a room in the cardiac area. After being checked out by several doctors, nurses, and others these are the facts and decisions to be made:

1. I had a heart attack. My heart had suffered damage.
2. I had several blockages, some up to 95 percent in major blood vessels surrounding my heart.
3. I required open heart surgery. I was in no condition to postpone it.
4. The plan, unless I objected, was to take me down for prep around eight and do surgery starting about nine in the morning. The surgery would take several hours.

5. They would take healthy blood vessels out of my legs and use them in my heart.
6. Get some rest.

Although, it was after three in the morning, what a wake-up call! *Suddenly, reality said hello.* I am fifty-three years old. I know my destiny, *but* I have children… My son was twenty-seven and married. My daughters were fifteen and sixteen, still in high school, needing their dad. Mom was healthy and seventy-seven. I have five siblings.

Wow, my mind was racing. My father had died of a heart attack, but he was sixty-eight. His father died of a heart attack at fifty-three. I remember praying, wanting to live, but not so much for myself, but for others in my life, especially my daughters.

Speaking with my son allowed me to voice concerns and make plans. I had things to do before they rolled me away.

First things first, shift change at work was at 4:00 a.m. I texted the supervisor, telling him I needed to speak with the night and day shift personnel at four. All must be present, including the guys from the tower. He promptly called me, asking what was going on… I assured him all was well, but some things had come up, and I wanted to talk with the team together one time.

At 4:00 a.m., I made the first of many calls. I asked if everyone was present and then asked to be put on speakerphone… I briefly explained the last ten hours to my coworkers and that I would have surgery shortly. I told them I'd keep them in the loop, and I appreciated each of them—"Stay safe. Take care of each other. God bless"—and I would see them soon.

The phone call was encouraging and a blessing, hearing my team wishing me well.

I later learned after I was off the phone the guys had a time of prayer for me.

I got a call shortly afterward from my friend Tony. He was not happy with me; I hadn't given him a heads-up when I first went to the hospital.

It was only the first of many calls I had to make. It wasn't going to get any easier. I called each of my siblings, waking them up, but was able to have good conversations with each of them. All said they would be praying for me, and we said, "I love yous."

The clock was ticking; surgery was coming. I needed to speak to my daughters. It is simple to say, oh, I could tell them I was going to be okay and that I love them. But what if this is the last time I got to speak to them? I called their mother, waking her, explaining what was going on. Thankfully, she was very strong and was good for the girls during this time. She woke up the girls; I did speak to them one at a time. I don't know what I said, but I wanted to encourage them, tell them they were special, and I loved them.

There was still one call to make. I needed to speak with my Mom. This was not going to be easy either. She was fit, sharp, lived by herself, and as noted earlier had just turned seventy-seven. I had called Uncle Charles, her dear brother, and a wonderful uncle, asking him to please be at her house at seven when I was going to call her.

By this time, my nurse was concerned with all the calls I was making. He said any stress was not good for me; he wanted the phone to disappear. I told him I was down to my last call. He shook his head but allowed me to make one last call.

I punched the numbers into the phone and hit send. Just as she picked up the phone and said hello, I could hear Uncle Charles coming through the garage door, calling to her, "That's Ron, and he's okay."

She said, "Ron, is this you?" and I said, "Good morning, Mom." She knew something was afoot, walked over, and sat down at the kitchen table, and Uncle Charles sat down beside her.

She asked what's going on. I told her about my heart attack and my pending surgery. Her voice told me she was numb, and thankfully, Uncle Charles was now holding her hand. I was worried about her, and she was hurting for me, remembering how my dad had passed. I did my best to reassure her I was going to be fine; I'd be back in touch soon. We said our goodbyes and our "I love yous." I knew before the phone was even disconnected; she was praying for me.

I needed a minute to relax, absorb all the calls. I could feel the strength of all those praying for me.

I talked with my son, thanking him for his help and for being there. I couldn't have asked any more of him. "I'm proud of you, and I love you. I'll see you soon." Then I was rolled away.

The next stop was surgical prep. Everyone was so serious, each attending to their job. A doctor stopped by, saying he was going to be the lead surgeon for my operation. He asked how I was doing.

I replied, "I'm ready." However, being totally honest, I added, "My dad had bypass surgery and never woke up. It's on my mind."

He told me, "Relax, you're going to be just fine."

I asked if we could pray together, and he said, "Absolutely." I prayed, and he smiled and gave me a shoulder squeeze of confidence.

As I waited, feeling alone, although there were many people nearby, I was praying, pleading for just ten years of life. Knowing that would get my daughters through college and able to stand on their own. A peace came over me, and I went to sleep.

Little did I know of all the activity going on in the background. Family was coming from out of town, the word was out, and so many were praying for me. My son was peppered with constant questions; he had been up all night, but no rest for the weary. Additionally, Fernando, our safety manager from work, was assigned to update those from work and even customers who were calling.

After hours of surgery, I was moved to recovery. I must have looked awful with tubes in my nose, down my throat, and three in my chest. IV bags hanging over both sides of my head. Then just as fast as I went to sleep, I was waking up. "Get this thing out of my mouth and throat." I was struggling to pull it out as the nurses came in and removed the ventilator. Comfortable again, I was back to sleep.

It wasn't much longer; I awoke to my former father-in-law and his wife standing in front of me. "Skip, is that you? Clara?" *They live over five hours away. What's going on? Am I hallucinating? He's a great guy, but here and now?*

Slowly, I was coming out of the anesthesia fog. My kids all passed through, smiling and giving me modified hugs. I was going to be okay… My first wife passed through, giving me a kiss on the forehead, saying, "I love you, Ron." Then my second wife stopped at my bedside moments later, leaning over, giving me a kiss on the forehead, saying, "I love you." Later in the day, my Mom popped in, as did my brother and older sister. I had to get better with all this love and encouragement.

My doctors assured me the surgery went well, and I was going to be okay. The next days showed me getting stronger. Moved out of ICU to a normal room, I was flooded with flowers and visitors. I was encouraged to walk a loop around the cardiac ward whenever I wanted, so I strolled in my gown, pushing the IV tower on wheels. However, this offended my daughter.

"Dad, your butt is hanging out."

I calmly replied, "Dear, sometimes it doesn't matter. I'm just happy to be walking."

After just a few days, I was making great progress. The doctor came in, asking if I was ready to go home. He said they wanted me out of the hospital before they made me sick. Absolutely, I was ready.

The Rest of the Story

I've been so blessed. The surgeon told me I should expect to live a normal life. My new cardiologist encouraged me to get back on the hardwood officiating basketball. When I hiked up from the bottom of the Grand Canyon a few years later, I sent her a postcard thanking her. Dr. Brenda was special.

My children have all grown into fine adults. I celebrated my ten-year anniversary in Oregon, when checking into my hotel room that night it was upgraded from a standard room to a king suite. Wow, *really*! The next day I hiked several miles of trails at Crater Lake National Park. Praise the Lord.

All, get your annual physicals, listen to your doctors, and encourage others to do the same.

Count your blessings and thank all those who pray for you.

"SIR, ARE YOU OKAY?"

The national parks in our country are fabulous, they each have their own uniqueness, Acadia to Zion. The travel bug was firmly planted in our family by my parents. As a military family, Dad was stationed around the country, Mom and Dad took us to parks and historical sites in the areas we lived. Most of the sites had free admission, especially for military personnel, so with all the children in tow we enjoyed many outings.

When Dad was stationed in San Diego, we would travel cross-country to visit our grandparents in Florida, riding in a Chevy station wagon without air conditioning. I can remember stopping at rest areas in the Southwest for lunch. When water was available at the picnic shelter, we'd strip down to our underwear and have a water party. Then the time when we asked for the crayons to color, Mom reached down retrieving the tin lunch box from the floorboard only to find all the crayons had melted into a multicolored soup.

As my children grew, we continued the tradition of getting out in nature visiting state and national parks. My dad passed way to early, but as I was a single parent, my mother quickly became a travel partner. Memories of travel with Granny are ingrained in the hearts of my children. She was always ready to go, adding laughter and joy on our journeys.

Eating on the road was always an adventure, you never knew if the diner was the right or wrong choice. We took a Conestoga wagon ride to a steak dinner in Yellowstone once. The steaks were great, but I failed to realize it was all you could eat although my teenage son told me multiple times and I was holding him back. When they finally made the last call for meat, he got another steak, and I got the "You never listen to me" look.

When on a ski vacation in Winter Park, I saw there was an Irish Mexican restaurant. We all boarded the shuttle bus; the driver asked us how we were doing and where we were heading. I proudly said we were going to the Irish Mexican Grill for dinner. He twice replied there is a good pizza place nearby, but my mind was set on Irish cuisine.

After a long slow dinner, nobody felt well, boarding the bus to return to our cabin we had the same driver. He asked how dinner was. We all said, "Bad! We should have had pizza." He just smiled, but we learned the lesson... Listen to the voice of experience.

Driving south through Wyoming everyone started getting hungry. We passed a couple of small towns with restaurants, I assured everyone looking at the map a much bigger town was about thirty-five to forty miles ahead. Big Piney would surely have a better choice of eateries. We drove into town, and there was only one option: the Chill Grill drive-in. *I don't think so.* We drove through town again and some back streets also—there was nothing else.

We pulled into a parking space, and a young girl only twelve or thirteen brought us menus. We reluctantly ordered burgers and fries. In just a few minutes, a younger boy (who couldn't have been ten) with a dirty face brought us our meals. Mom had already decided she would pass on eating. We blessed the food and began eating the most wonderful hamburgers. Mom, hearing us, decided to join us. If I ever get back to Big Piney, I'm heading to the Chill Grill for a burger.

When my oldest daughter graduated from the University of Florida, I planned a father-daughter trip to several national parks to celebrate. The focus was to get into the outdoors and do some hiking together.

The anticipated highlight of the trip was an overnight at Phantom Ranch. Where and what is Phantom Ranch? After more than six months of trying, I finally secured reservations at the bottom of the Grand Canyon. The ranch is just a short stroll off the Colorado River. It features a handful of cabins, men's and women's bunkhouses, and a canteen.

It was mid-May, but the temperature was a brisk thirty-seven degrees as we left our hotel and headed to the bus stop. Thinking about what lay ahead, I couldn't help flashing back to a hike of the Panoramic Trail in Yosemite National Park just two years previous. We were ill-prepared and did not bring enough water. When standing to exit the shuttle bus after completing the hike, my whole body became one large cramp. I was hurting all over as I literally shuffled to the door and had to sit down once off the bus.

Being from Florida, the cool weather had me wanting to add more layers of clothing, but that would change soon. The shuttle bus arrived, we headed to the South Kaibab trailhead. It was almost seven in the morning as we set off down the trail. Soon we reached Ooh Aah Point, the vast canyon just seemed to open before us. The colors in the early part of the day were amazing and had me saying "Ooh! Aah!" too.

Three miles down the trail we arrived at Cedar Ridge we got a reminder to hydrate. Friends of a hiker were pleading with the handler of a mule supply train to take their buddy back to the trailhead. He had drunk too much alcohol the night before. "Rest, hydrate," was the advice as the heat of the day was coming.

Further down the trail with the first views of the Colorado River we stopped for lunch. My daughter was quickly introduced to a pesky squirrel. He was determined to share her lunch and she was not about to allow it. Definitely, lunch with a view.

Upon reaching the river, you realize looking around you can't see anything but canyon and your thousands of feet down from the rim. I was tired but happy to reach the bridge, cross the river, but where was Phantom Ranch? Not there yet, must keep strolling.

We arrived at Phantom Ranch and were not disappointed, quaint rock cabins, Bright Angel Creek flowing nearby, where a few hikers were relaxing in the cool water. The specialty at the canteen is lemonade, absolutely the best lemonade ever. I sat in the cool of the building and enjoyed at least four large glasses of the tart sweet goodness. Hydration was never so enjoyable.

After a long shower and a bountiful dinner, I had no problem sleeping. A wake-up call came to the bunkhouse via a hard knocking on the door at 5:00 a.m., the first breakfast was served at 5:30 a.m. This was the beginning of a long, long day. We were assigned to the second sitting, so we had daylight as we grabbed our lunches, and said goodbye to a unique habitation.

We crossed the suspension bridge; five thousand feet of elevation gain and nine miles of the Bright Angel Trail lay ahead. Truth be known my body was stiff and hurting, let's hope I loosen up. We were soon passed by four young women all wearing Ohio State gear. I couldn't help but chide them. This made for trail fun as we passed each other several times and more than once they spelled out *O-H-I-O* for me.

On arrival at Indian Garden, we passed the Buckeye ladies for the final time. Under hydrated, a couple of them were suffering with cramps and we were still roughly five miles below the rim. We wished them well and moved on after some snacks.

After leaving Indian Garden, I caught a second breath, began moving well, but then we arrived at the Devil's Corkscrew. This is a series of switchbacks designed to kick hiker butt. I had completed Walter's Wiggles on Angel's Landing just a week before but, *wow*, the Corkscrew got the best of me. A lot of water and rest breaks got me through. Still miles to trails end.

As we got further up the trail, we began interfacing with a lot of day hikers, some with limited or no water, others with poor footwear (including flip-flops). I was encouraging many as we would pass them, but it was more of a ruse, as I was trying too pump-up myself.

Then it happened, my daughter turned to me, knowing I was struggling, saying "You can do this, Dad!"

Grumpy, tired, and exhausted, I blasted back, saying, I didn't want to hear it. She fired back, calling me a hypocrite, encouraging others but not wanting to hear it. We walked in silence for a while.

One lesson learned walking out of the canyon: don't be looking up searching for the rim. There are so many turns, so what you think is the rim is just the top of another bluff as you continue upward. I remembered reading very near the trailhead was a tunnel or arch, looking ahead it could see it in the distance. I was so excited thinking that the end was near, picking up my snail-like pace. My daughter was happy I was moving better. Upon reaching the tunnel, all I could see was trail and more switchbacks in the distance.

No! No! No! Finding a rock to sit on, I got out my trail map only to discover there are two tunnels on the trail. Although we were closer, there was still a way to go. I wanted to scream. Fortunately, my daughter was there. I just sat. Then she bribed me.

We had heard at Phantom Ranch, just as we enjoyed the lemonade, that at the rim was the ice cream shop, a great ending point. At Indian Garden, someone mentioned it serving big scoops of cold deliciousness. "Dad, it's only three quarters of a mile to the ice cream shop. What flavor do you want?" We started talking ice cream, and I began to move again. As we walked, my parched mouth was watering, my focus became sitting in shade enjoying scoops of ice cream.

Before long, we were at the second tunnel. I had caught a glimpse of a building; the end was near. Finally, the trailhead. *Thank You, Lord!* I said a brief prayer, threw my hands in the air, and hugged my daughter. "Let's go get some ice cream!"

Reminder, we had just hiked nine miles, with five thousand feet of elevation gain; it was the second of two long days. I was exhausted, sweating, in need of a long shower. While trying to locate the ice cream shop, we ended up in the parking lot of a hotel. Seeing some of the housekeeping staff, I approached them to inquire where the ice cream shop was.

A woman, who was obviously a manager, stopped me before I could speak. "Sir, are you okay?" I ignored her question, saying something about ice cream. Forcefully, out shot her hand, interrupting me, giving me the stop sign. Then, much louder with emphasis, she repeated, "Sir, are you okay?"

I immediately stopped and said yes. I explained we had just finished hiking up from Phantom Ranch, was very tired but okay, and was looking for the infamous ice cream shop. I've often wondered how rough I must have looked, but I've grown to appreciate her caring about me, a complete stranger.

We made it to the ice cream shop; there was no line, cool air was blowing, two big scoops please. We found a nice spot on the wall overlooking the canyon, sat down, thinking we'd enjoy the moment. Not so fast.

While relaxing, talking about how refreshing the ice cream was, and reflecting on the last two days, a group of tourists disturbed our peace, compounding the issue. A few of them were acting like they were tossing food to a squirrel in our general direction. The squirrel was scrambling and confused as he couldn't find the snacks being tossed to him. He studied us like we were involved in denying him his treat.

Then, seeing my daughter's open backpack, he charged forward, across my daughter's lap into her pack. She jumped, yelled, kicked, almost dropping her ice cream, and gave the death stare to the tourists. They quickly backed away, thankfully, no one laughed, or they may have seen her head spin.

After finishing the refreshing ice cream, we boarded the shuttle bus to head back to our hotel. Normally, the buses are full, people packed together, strangely no one wanted to sit beside me. I guess there are advantages to hiking.

We exited the bus, still having a third of a mile to reach our room. There was a slight grade uphill, but my body wanted no part of it. About a hundred yards from home, I could feel the cramps coming, legs, arms, and abdomen. Fighting through them, I reached the room and collapsed on my bed to await my turn in the shower.

What an incredible two days, viewing creation at its best. The two trails brought out the best in us (some grumpiness in me). That night at dinner, we laughed at each other, recalled the toughest parts, and agreed we'd always hold onto this special memory.

Family travel is memorable at all ages. You can go from being an "Are we there yet?" child to being the parent organizing and learning to roll with the "Oh nos!" and "Oh mys!" Visiting the Grand Canyon is an awesome journey that should be on your family adventure list. Don't wait. Start planning and packing the car!

IT IS WELL

As I wrote this book, I was constantly reminded that when I look at my life, so many amazing things have occurred. This book only contains a portion of the stories. I wanted to share a few more and recognize some special people before closing the book.

Very late one night, driving home from college (Miami to Central Florida), I drove many miles on the wrong side of a four-lane divided highway. When a semi-tractor-trailer finally got my attention, I returned to the correct side of the roadway. Within seconds, police cars came onto the scene with lights flashing, obviously looking for me.

The hitchhiker I picked up outside of Gainesville early one evening, as I was headed to Miami, provided a memorable experience. Having a good discussion, I talked him into joining me for supper, after about eighty miles. We stopped at my parent's home, had a good meal, and were back on the road.

About another hour down the road, he mentioned he had been a jailed felon. He had done time in several Florida state prisons but hated Sumter Correctional. The admin, guards, and overall situation were awful, he despised them, all but threatening the personnel. My father's freshly ironed prison guard uniform for Sumter Correctional was hanging on the kitchen divider while we had supper. How was he blind to it? Or was he unable to react to it? We drove several hours to Miami. He asked to be let out just as we arrived at the city outskirts, thanking and wishing me well.

Two summers, I got to attend Royal Ambassador (RA) camp for a week. A man from our church paid for me to attend. Later, when my dad retired and we were relocating, the gentleman gave me his New Testament, which I still have.

Miriam and Marvin Fussell were so special to our family when we moved to Central Florida. Their five children were about the same age as us. She was a hairstylist; he was a farmer. Each one of us kids worked in the fields for them. It allowed us to earn some money as we were starting high school. The friendships built, lessons learned, and money earned were priceless as I look back.

I must mention the Class of 1968 at Webster Junior High School. The one year I attended radically changed my life. I went from a poor student to the honor roll. Many of the students in that one-room class are still making major impacts on their communities many decades later. I was blessed with lifelong friends who are just good people. Met my first girlfriend. Future college roommates were in the class. I want to list the names of all those special classmates, but I'd be ashamed if I missed even one. Let me mention two special encouragers: Danny McCoy, the science teacher; and Sam Harris, the school principal. They both also followed us to the high school.

All through my life, the right people have mentored, assisted, or just been good friends. Lynwood Irby, Mike Clayton, Dave Lawson, Chris Patrick, Sonny Hirsch, the entire FEC Quarry Loadout Team, Tony Valdes, Yolanda Cook-Robeson, Ralph Pollard, Wayne Blaylock, R. C. Moore, several pastors, and the South Broward Gideons. My brother and all four sisters. So many others, this list could go on.

I entitled this story "It Is Well" because I've been watched over in many ways and through so many circumstances. Maybe the book should have been titled "A Truly Blessed Life."

I want to close the book with the words of an old hymn:

> When upon life's billows you are tempest tossed
> When you are discouraged thinking all is lost
> Count your many blessings name them one by
>   one
> And it will surprise you what the Lord has done.
> Count your blessings; name them one by one
> Count your many blessing; see what God has
>   done.

I still have many years to live. What adventures and amazing occurrences lie ahead? I'm counting my blessings. WHAT! WOW! REALLY!

ARE YOU KIDDING ME?

ABOUT THE AUTHOR

Ron Hart is a father and grandfather living in South Florida. After a decade of sports experiences, Ron had a long career working in safety, distribution by rail and truck, and team building with a prominent aggregates company. Currently staying active with church activities, The Gideons International, and getting out in nature to enjoy this beautiful world.